MODERN POETRY OF PAKISTAN

MODERN POETRY OF PAKISTAN

EDITED BY IFTIKHAR ARIF

TRANSLATIONS EDITED BY WAQAS KHWAJA

DALKEY ARCHIVE PRESS

CHAMPAIGN AND LONDON

Library of Congress Cataloging-in-Publication Data

Modern poetry of Pakistan / edited by Iftikhar Arif ; translations edited by Waqas Khwaja. -- 1st ed.
p. cm.
Includes poems translated from seven major languages in Pakistan:
Balochi, Kashmiri, Punjabi, Pashto, Seraiki, Sindhi, and Urdu.
ISBN 978-1-56478-605-0 (pbk. : alk. paper)
1. Pakistani poetry--20th century--Translations into English. I. Iftikhar, Arif. II. Khwaja, Waqas Ahmad.
PK2978.E5M65 2011
808.81'0089914122--dc22
2010035342

The publication of *Modern Poetry of Pakistan* was made possible by support from
the University of Illinois at Urbana-Champaign, as well as by grants from the National
Endowment for the Arts, a federal agency, and the Illinois Arts Council, a state agency.

Permission for use of the poems has been granted by the copyright holders.

www.dalkeyarchive.com

Cover image: "Incense Burner." Acrylic on wood. 30 x 30 in. Copyright © 2006 by Lubna Agha.
Used with kind permission of the artist. Design and composition by Danielle Dutton.
Printed on permanent/durable acid-free paper and bound in the United States of America.

CONTENTS

Poetry is universal, and its enduring appeal depends on the ability of poets to capture and convey our innermost emotions. Like a fragrance that spreads everywhere in a subtle, almost imperceptible way, poetry transcends all borders and nationalities. Pakistani poetry is especially rich because it is inspired by the mystic poets of Sufi tradition. Indeed, the fundamental ethos of Pakistani culture and literature is perhaps most visible in the Sufi poetry of the region. The mystics lived their lives among the common people, giving expression to their sorrows and joys. Their poetry is an open rebellion against prejudice, intolerance, and hatred. This mystic heritage, which is reflected in all the country's regional languages, is the driving force behind Pakistani poetry.

The subject matter of Pakistani poetry ranges from romance to resistance against the tyranny of dictators and other oppressors. Some of our more traditional poetry is couched in rhyme and meter, while some is free verse. The most recent Pakistani poetry is offbeat and avant-garde and exudes a new sensibility, infused with fresh metaphors and similes. As a general rule, though, the diction of our poetry is devoid of stereotypes, clichés, and other hackneyed expressions. Pakistani poetry can, I believe, easily be compared to the best poetry currently being written in any of the world's major languages.

I hope that this selection of poems will provide a comprehensive glimpse into the vibrant literature of Pakistan. I am sure that American readers will be both surprised and delighted by the kaleidoscopic colors of our country's poetry.

I offer my appreciation to the American Embassy in Pakistan for arranging reciprocal translations of the poetry of our two countries.

FAKHAR ZAMAN
Chairman, Pakistan Academy of Letters, Islamabad

The poetry of Pakistan is not something young like the country, which is only some six decades old. It represents an unbroken tradition rooted in the rich mystic soil of the land and in the refined and highly sophisticated verse of masters like Meer, Ghalib, and Iqbal, whose own sources of inspiration go back to the great Persian poets Hafiz, Saadi, Rumi, and Omar Khayyam. It is by no means a matter of opinion when I say that the heritage of world literature has been the poorer for not having given due recognition to this magnificent tradition, but I would hasten to add that the fault has entirely been our own for not endeavoring to facilitate translations of this work into the major languages of the world.

We are a multilingual country, one in which a host of cultures, intermingled with folk traditions that have persisted for millennia, informs the national psyche and colors creative expression in all its various forms. Pakistani literature itself spans a broad range, its themes encompassing moral, social, emotional, intellectual, and philosophical issues. In the realm of poetry, the topic of love, with its limitless dimensions, of course claims the largest territory, yet reflections and insights abound concerning society and the human condition, particularly in regard to the question of how the individual braves the privations of a developing economy while tradition grapples with new ideas. In Pakistan, modern trends in poetry have been evident almost from the advent of modernity itself: it would be difficult to single out any "experimental" trend in Western poetry that has failed to find enthusiasts among the younger generation of our own poets as well (sometimes to the great amusement of the classical school). In our own literary milieu, debates still rage between the art-for-art's-sake school and those who argue that art must serve society:the progressive movement, which originated in the 1920s, in the wake of the Bolshevik Revolution, and which held sway for close to a half century, continues to be visible in certain areas of mainstream poetry, if no longer as strident as it once was. Faiz Ahmad Faiz, Ahmad Nadeem Qasmi, Sheikh Ayaz, and Gul Khan Naseer were among the last great progressives.

The creation of Pakistan in 1947 provided space for a synthesis of the intellectual and philosophical thought that emerged on the Indian subcontinent following the arrival of Muslims in the eighth century. During the centuries preceding the birth of Pakistan, Islamic thought had undergone a number of important developments, represented by such luminaries as Amir Khusro (1253–1325); Sheikh Ahmad Sarhindi, known as Mujaddid Alif Thani (1564–1624); Shah Waliullah (1703–1762); and Sir Syed Ahmad Khan (1817–1898). This process found its fullest expression in the thought and poetry of Allama Muhammad Iqbal (1877–1938), who spearheaded the move in British India for an independent Muslim state. His poetry and thought have influenced successive generations of poets and thinkers, not only on the subcontinent but throughout the Muslim world.

Among the poets who became popular in the new country were N. M. Rashid, Meeraji, and Faiz Ahmad Faiz. This troika represents three divergent trends in Urdu poetry: Faiz's inspiration coming from progressive Marxist ideology, whereas Rashid and Meeraji represent the modernists. Nasir Kazmi captured the experience of migration, combining the classical with a highly contemporary sensibility, while Majeed Amjad made creative use of local imagery and idiom. Others, among them Qaiyyum Nazar, Mukhtar Siddiqi, Zia Jalandhari, Yousaf Zafar, Aziz Hamid Madni, and Saqi Faruqi, gave new vigor to the Urdu *nazm*, and Jamiluddin Aali, Ahmad Faraz, Athar Nafees, and Jaun

Elia did the same for the Urdu *ghazal*. With their unique styles and vision, poets such as Ahmad Nadeem Qasmi, Munir Niazi, Saleem Ahmad, and Zafar Iqbal have given us new ways of looking at the world. Similarly, Ghani Khan, Janbaz Jatoi, Taos Banihali, and Sheikh Ayaz have opened up new paths for poets writing in Pashto, Seraiki, Kashmiri, and Sindhi.

A distinctive blend of Arabic vocabulary, Persian epic tone, and the echoes of a historic past finds expression in many a talented poet of our time. Akhtar Hussain Ja'afri combined these elements into a coherent system of thought, producing a small volume of poetry that stands out for its virtuosity. Along with my contemporaries, I have also made my humble contribution to this classical mode. More recently, another trend has emerged in which the epic tone of the Persian classics is being transposed into a highly modern atmosphere. Over the course of the twentieth century, prose poetry also matured and became the preferred form of many gifted poets, including Abdul Rashid, Qamar Jamil, Ahmad Hamesh, and Mubarak Ahmad.

The work of women poets has become increasingly multidimensional as they explore and expose the world that appears to their eyes. Never before in our history have we seen such a large number of women writers and poets contributing so significantly to our literature: Ada Jaffery, Zehra Nigah, Kishwar Naheed, Fahmida Riaz, Parveen Shakir, Shahida Hasan, and Yasmeen Hameed to name but a few.

Poetry is not just something to be read, but, like music, is a popular passion in Pakistan—people come in the thousands to listen to poets recite their verses. Quite a few of our poets have excellent singing voices and have developed melodies of their own in which to sing their work, crooning their compositions to cries of "Mukarrer, mukarrer!" ("Encore, encore!"). New collections of poetry are launched in one city or another nearly every day—but, in the end, the current volume had to limit itself to forty-four poets only. Even if one were to restrict one's selection to living poets only, and be utterly uncompromising in this selection, working with so small a number would have been a difficult task at best; to make one's selection from across the entire twentieth century, however, from all the major languages of Pakistan—Urdu, Punjabi,

Sindhi, Pashto, Balochi, Seraiki, and Kashmiri—and from the entire range of progressives, modernists, classicists, formalists, and so on, was an exercise in aesthetic brutality. I have had to make hard-to-justify omissions from every class of poets. Yet, from even this relatively small sample, I feel the Western reader will still gain an appreciation of the poetic output of Pakistan and its representative variety—the remarkable range of poetic sentiments, thoughts, and themes.

Giving shape to the idea of presenting the poetry of our two countries in companion volumes of English and Urdu translations has been a very fulfilling and exciting experience. I am aware of how hard the translators must have worked in order to capture at least the essence of the original poems, even where precise cultural equivalents might not have been easy to come by. I hope that this exchange will continue, and even be expanded, in the coming years. I am grateful to Dana Gioia, the former chairman of the National Endowment for the Arts in the United States, and to the Ministry of Education and the Ministry of Culture here in Pakistan for supporting this immensely valuable project.

IFTIKHAR ARIF
Chairman, National Language Authority, Islamabad
Former Chairman, Pakistan Academy of Letters, Islamabad

Stirring Up a Vespiary

We inhabit a world of translations. All around us, at all times, everything is changing, renewing itself. Things are constantly transforming, transmuting into something else, conveying life to one already evolving form by giving up their body and essence in another. We use language of all kinds—written, oral, visual, tactile, aural, mathematical—to translate our thoughts, impressions, calculations, and feelings, to find expression for what seeks articulation and communication. The striving to render our thoughts, feelings, and emotions into recognizable shape, into legible characters, into comprehensible, com- municable speech or discourse lies at the heart of our experience of a lived life. The translations continue in our sleeping and waking hours, whether we will it or not, at times when our consciousness is alert and in moments of vacancy and reflection. Translation is a state natural to us, natural to our existence. Is it any wonder, then, that in such a world of continual transformations, some of us engage in the process of conducting the form, sensibility, and sense of one language into another, the texts of one language into the matrices of another?

Yet it is widely recognized that literary translation is impossible, that as Tony Barnstone puts it, "all translation is mistranslation," that we can ren- der the original only in a version that is something other than the original

(T. Barnstone 11). We do not necessarily need reinforcement of this idea from linguists and deconstructionists to acknowledge its truth. What we also know is that we engage in translations, literary and other, nonetheless. The arc of our ambition may be somewhat abbreviated, as with W. S. Merwin who suggests that "without deliberately altering the overt meaning of the original poem, I wanted the translation to represent, with as much life as possible, some aspect, some quality of the poem that made the translator think it was worth translating in the first place," or in the case of Ok-Koo Kang Grosjean, for whom translation tries to capture "the *rasa*, or flavor, of the poetry," rather than attempt fidelity to the original in a literal sense (Merwin 155, Grosjean 65). But translations are not abandoned just because they are "impossible" to do. In fact, this may precisely be the reason why the exercise fascinates so many poets and translators. "Is translation of poetry possible?" asks Willis Barnstone, the first translator of Mao's poems into English. "Of course not," he responds to his own question, and goes on to add, "It is impossible. And it should be understood that only the difficult, the elusive, the impossible lines are worth translating" (W. Barnstone 34).

In charting his evolution as a translator and the contours of his translation process, Willis Barnstone offers a useful preliminary plan for would-be translators (and translation editors, for that matter):

> When I began to translate, I believed, as I do now, that fidelity to the poem meant creating a poem in English, a good poem, one that a poet (or, at the very least, one who is a poet in the act of re-creation) translates. To do this requires freedom, perhaps a lot of freedom. But as I have gotten older, my view has changed. I think now that one should try to be as close as possible to the literal meaning, but not in a clumsy way. Within that closeness, and aided by an immense amount of information provided by the fullest knowledge of that literal meaning (with all its connotative elements and music), one can operate with great artistic privilege. Like reproducing formal prosody, to be close is hard but saves one from being seduced by the obvious. Therefore, one is obliged to come up with ten or twenty solutions for

each linguistic enigma, one must take greater imaginative leaps, and in the end, I believe, this allows the original poet to talk. (W. Barnstone 32–33)

There is, however, in the strategy suggested by Barnstone's evolving view of translation, a lurking danger spawned by the phenomenon of poet-translators who do not know the language from which they translate and rely instead on accidental native informants, narrow, often under-prepared academics, handy dictionaries and grammars, and even on other translations to help them make sense of the originals. The original may then come to be viewed primarily as an excuse for the work offered as a translation—a translation influenced (as it inevitably is) by the qualifications and quality of the native informants, the isolation of words from their colloquial use and context, the unfamiliarity with literary tradition and conventions, and the lack of experiential understanding of the original's field of nuance and connotation. No wonder translators operating under these conditions would want to claim greater creative freedom in translation and be prone to indulging themselves in the name of art.

A significant number of translators have succumbed to the seduction of this indulgence. Willis Barnstone's son, Tony Barnstone—himself also a translator of Chinese poetry—observes: "From the early metrical and end-rhymed translations of Herbert Giles to the so-called free-verse translations of Ezra Pound, Arthur Waley, and Kenneth Rexroth, Chinese poems have been reinvented as American poems" (T. Barnstone 2). Later, in the same essay, he notes: "I have argued elsewhere that Chinese poetry in English has deviated deeply from the form, aesthetics, and concerns of the Chinese originals and that this is the result of willful mistranslation by modernist and postmodern poet-translators" (10). Pertinently, W. S. Merwin reminds us that throughout the nineteenth century the "notion of what translation really was or could be [was] undergoing a change . . . partly as a result of efforts to bring over into English a growing range and variety of originals" (Merwin 152).

The trend Merwin identifies brings up yet another area of concern—the imperial absorption of texts from other parts of the world into the colonial language, whether in the name of scholarship or as a source of entertainment for the reading public, consciously or unconsciously complicit with the project of empire building, and the underlying belief that, the *essence* engrossed in the translation, there was no more need or value for the original anymore. Whether it is Sir William Jones rendering texts from Sanskrit, Persian, or Arabic into English, Edward Fitzgerald rewriting the *Rubaiyat* of Omar Khayyam, or Pound working his "translucences" of Chinese poems from the notes left by Ernest Fenollosa (who knew almost no Chinese himself), there is something offensive to a native speaker of those languages in the attitude that informs these exercises. However much the translations may have contributed to the development of poetry in the language of translation, such reworking remains an act of intervention, subversion, and appropriation, especially when firsthand knowledge of and fidelity to the original become matters of remote interest, if any at all. When presumptions that the translation has improved upon the original, and, afforded the opportunity, that poets of the language of translation can exceed in design, theme, and accomplishment the achievements of the poets translated, are added to this lack of cultural, contextual, and linguistic immediacy or understanding, the matter becomes laughable indeed.

Ironically, translations based on library-confined self-learning or on the misreading of texts paraphrased by accidental native informers have been known to inspire entirely new fashions and trends in the poetry of the language of translation. "All translation is mistranslation," Tony Barnstone declares, "but a translator's work and joy are to rig, out of the materials at hand, something that opens cans, or carries hay, or sends voices through the lines. We will never create a truly Chinese poem in English, but in this way we can extend the possibilities of the translation, which may in turn reveal to the imaginations of American poets unforeseen continents" (T. Barnstone 11). W. S. Merwin writes about the Chinese translations of Waley and Pound in the same vein: "Their relations to the forms and the life of the originals I will never be able to assess. But from the originals, by means and aspirations that were, in certain respects, quite new, they made something new in English and they revealed a whole new range of possibility for poetry in English. Poetry in our language has never been the same since, and all of us are indebted to Waley and Pound whether we recognize and acknowledge it or not" (Merwin 152).

Such remarks are a study in the kind of appropriating impulse I have noted. Merwin seems reluctant to acknowledge any debt to the original Chinese poets. It is Waley and Pound's "means and aspirations" (which, to his mind, are "in certain respects, quite new") that have opened up a "whole new range of possibility in English poetry," and our gratitude should accordingly be addressed to them. In the end, it matters little what the original Chinese poems are, how they function, or what their forms and strategies of composition are. They have been impressionistically absorbed by Waley and Pound and turned into English poems, and this has given English poetry a momentous charge to diversify in directions hitherto unknown to it.

Two hundred and thirty years earlier, Sir William Jones had translated poems from Arabic, Persian, and Sanskrit, partly with a similar hope of opening up new possibilities for European poetry. His work inspired a raging trend of "orientalist" poetry and prose in England (it had its effect in continental Europe as well), contributing significantly towards kindling the Romantic movement and keeping it stoked. A skilled philologist, Jones had learned the languages from which he translated. He spent the last eleven years of his relatively brief life (he died at forty-seven) in Calcutta engaged in scholarly work, in addition to his official duties as puisne judge of the Supreme Court of Bengal. He had a deep respect for the ancient and classical texts of these Oriental languages, and his eagerness to see in them a source of replenishment for European literary tradition is quite understandable. But, in the final analysis, despite his very genuine admiration for the literary achievements of the East, even he could not shed the propensity to look at that literature as a vehicle for what it might offer in terms of poetic possibilities to the literature of the West. He concludes his famous essay "On the Poetry of the Eastern Nations" (1772) with the following caveats and proposals:

> I must once more request, that, bestowing these praises on the writings of *Asia*, I may not be thought to derogate from the merit of the *Greek* and *Latin* poems, which have justly been admired in every age; yet I cannot but think that our *European* poetry has subsisted too long on the perpetual repetition of the same images, and incessant

allusions to the same fables: and it has been my endeavour for several years to inculcate this truth, *That, if the principal writings of the Asiaticks, which are reposited in our publick libraries, were printed with the usual advantage of notes and illustrations, and if the languages of the Eastern nations were studied in our places of education, where every other branch of useful knowledge is taught to perfection, a new and ample field would be open for speculation; we should have a more extensive insight into the history of the human mind, we should be furnished with a new set of images and similitudes, and a number of excellent compositions would be brought to light, which future scholars might explain, and future poets might imitate.* (Jones 228–29)

There is nothing wrong with this agenda on the face of it; in fact, it would even be laudable were it to operate as part of a voluntary and disinterested exchange on all sides, so that all parties could appreciate each other's literary productions and learn of new creative and aesthetic strategies from each other. But the agenda could be, and was, all too easily appropriated by the empire builders of the day for their imperial project, not forgetting the proud claim that in their institutions of learning "*every other branch of useful knowledge is taught to perfection.*" Perhaps this complicity is built into the assumptions that undergird Jones's proposal, for he is so caught in his fascination for the past literary "excellences" of England's newly acquired territories that he disregards, or dismisses, contemporary literary production and activity in them. This neglect might have been less troublesome had it not coincided with the conclusion that these cultures were no longer vibrant and that the populations of these territories were therefore in need of suitable oversight. But there is the sense that the past literature, beliefs, and customs of the colonized peoples offer a means of control over them in that the person who gains this knowledge comes so thoroughly to understand these subjectivized peoples that he acquires also the right to legislate for them and determine categorically what may be good or bad for them. In his nine hymns to various Hindu gods and goddesses (Camdeo, Durga, Bhavani, Indra, Surya, Lacshimi, Narayena, Sereswaty, and Ganga), for instance, Jones often adopts the persona of a venerable Hindu poet who, after rehearsing the ancient wisdom of Hindu tradition, invariably endorses British rule in India as the condition, and hope, for its future success and prosperity. Michael J. Franklin correctly points out the "intended metropolitan destination [London] and propagandist purposes of these odes." Noting Jones's opposition to civil liberty and free government in India and his support of absolute rule and preservation of local laws and customs, Franklin also recognizes in this stance "a nexus of responsibilities not wholly dissimilar from what a century later became known as 'the white man's burden'" (Franklin 64). Thus, even a translator as dedicated and tireless as Sir William Jones was not above disregarding the contemporary context and apt, at the same time, to assume an understanding of the "native" speaker, its historical motivations, and its inclinations, that was superior to the "native's" own self-apprehension or self-knowledge.

What, then, does literary translation involve? How, despite what are seen as virtually insurmountable odds, can translation happen so that it does not undervalue, misrepresent, or (not an unknown phenomenon) utterly dispense with the original? The arrogation of both the privilege and power to translate into English often works in one direction, to the detriment of the text translated. Given the dominance of English and Euro-American institutions of production, dissemination, and interpretation as a natural historical fallout of Western imperialism, the determination of methodology and meaning lies essentially with the new centers of power in the West—academic institutions, university and commercial presses, print, visual, and digital media. The reverse is also true: literary and translation theory in, and translation of English texts into, regional and local languages of former colonies have neither the exposure nor the authority of their privileged Western counterparts. As a consequence, there is no real conversation or dialogue, by which I mean conversation and dialogue on the basis of parity, between the two sides that are inevitably crucial to the translation process. How can a translator ensure that the text being translated is accorded respect for its own sake, and on its own terms? Should the drive to find exotic avenues of development for the poetry of one's own language and culture (and/or for one's own work) override the responsibility one owes, when undertaking what one claims to be a translation, to transmit with fidelity a text from another language? Can literary translation be approached only in extremes, either creatively or literally? Is there no way of combining the two, no way to pursue what Ok-Koo Kang Grosjean calls the "middle way"?

A good translator is an exquisite ambassador. Just as the creative artist suggests new ways of looking at the commonplace, the translator opens up to readers a whole new world, a whole new mode of perception and experience, they may hardly have suspected of existing. Although language is primarily a means of communication, with usage and exchange it acquires over a period the sensibility peculiar to the people that transact it, one that is, in many ways, itself dictated by the physical environment and material conditions of the language's provenance and prevalence. This sensibility seems seldom, if ever, to be interchangeable between languages. The function of a translator, to my mind, is to find approximations that do the least violence to the original work while preserving to the greatest possible extent its significations and design. Since it is not always possible to find such solutions, the translator must also be creative and be able to produce a recognizable flavor (*rasa*) where the full taste of the original is not transferable.

As form and cadence, too, are exclusive to each language, they further complicate the task of a translator. All too little account may be taken of the social and material conditions that, in some way or another, impinge upon a work of literature and upon language itself. Neither conceptual paradigms nor languages remain static or immutable, for practice and performance are constantly modifying them. Assorted vernaculars, dialects, and hybrids exist in distinct, yet interwoven, strains. An excessively close and sensitive reading may overdistinguish the subtle currents in the stream that conveys thoughts from one point to another, while an overly rigorous objective distancing may produce the illusion of homogeneity. We may tend to weight words and images with meanings they presently carry and so, we believe, must always have carried. We may also interpret behavioral patterns in the context of our current sociocultural background, understanding, and expectations, just as, in reverse, we may impose specific motives and intentions, picked up from our own reading, on situations and formulations that deserve to be appreciated with an open mind. Where, in translation, a clash of sensibilities occurs, or inadequate attention is paid to historical and cultural displacement, the result is liable to become banal, odd, or even ludicrous. It is a perilous process then, this translation, and one that succeeds less often than is generally assumed.

Yet there is this great need, felt both individually and collectively, to share, to transmit, and to translate from one language to another. Translation is a kind of recoding, a mapping of one language system onto another. In a sense, recoding is itself a re-creation and so can never be the duplicate of the original; the result is bound always to be more or less. But this recoding may also provide recreation, a *diversion*—a turning aside, an amusement, the pleasure of play. Our deep-seated impulse to retell stories, with subtle shifts of emphasis (whether conscious or unconscious), a readjusted point of view, or in a reimagined form, may be another abetting factor. There are also the more obvious reasons, apparently simpler, but potentially as dangerous in the way they negotiate the original, and equally as important in their effect: to make accessible to foreign audiences the literature of a specific area, to convey the significance and stature of its artistic productions, to have these works become part of the international discourse of literary classics, itself a notoriously vexed subject. Below the surface, it is the old excitement of dismantling and deconstructing and the lure of reassembling and redesigning. A good literary translation perhaps looks for a happy marriage between these two competing impulses: the transference from one language to another and re-creation of the text. Translations, as transactions between languages, are thus important in more ways than one. They help to develop individual languages at the same time that they exchange or transfer patterns of perception, imagery, formal structures of expression, and organization of material.

The present anthology contains translations into English of 148 poems from seven major languages of Pakistan, six of them regional (Balochi, Kashmiri, Punjabi, Pashto, Seraiki, and Sindhi) and one national (Urdu). It represents the work of forty-four poets and fifteen translators. When I was invited, in November 2007, to take up the responsibility of translation editor for this volume, I was both daunted and, somewhat apprehensively, thrilled. Nothing of this kind, to my knowledge, had previously been attempted in the United States. There are volumes of translations of individual poets, as well as collections that present the poetry of one particular language or another, but not an anthology showcasing poems from so many different languages from one particular country.

The reach of the anthology, the effort to represent the poetry of all of modern Pakistan, creates a challenging problem in selection. Over the past half a century, a vast amount of poetry has been produced in the country's many languages. As anyone familiar with this output would realize, strong disagreements could exist about whom to include in such a volume. No matter what the selection process, questions would remain, for any editor brings his or her biases to the work. Iftikhar Arif, then Chairman of the Pakistan Academy of Letters, made the selections for this anthology, and they reflect the mood of his times, the temper and temperament of officialdom in a military-supervised democracy. Far from vitiating the project, this in fact makes it more noteworthy. These are the poems of a society riven by ethnic, class, sectarian, and political differences, yet there is an attempt to show that the poems in these various languages are all of a piece, that they belong to the same culture and share many similar concerns and perceptions.

The selection of poets and poems having already been made, I felt free to concentrate on arranging for the work of translation. I have thus been engaged these last couple of years in securing, what to my mind appeared, the best possible translations of poems that sometimes seemed impossible to render into English or whose field of allusion and experience defied easy transference across linguistic boundaries. Having looked through existing translations of poetry from some of the languages included here, and having considered the nature of the reservations I had about them, I decided early that I would try to get the translations done by people who were not only familiar with the idiom, historical background, and cultural context of the language of composition but almost, if not equally, as comfortable with these markers in the language of translation. This was an exacting requirement, and it did not always bear fruit. Although I had intended to have a series of translators do anywhere from five to ten poems each, it did not quite work out that way, and, in the end, I found myself taking on around one third of the translations myself. Good translators are not easy to find and once found are not always eager to embark on fresh translations.

I grew up speaking Urdu, Punjabi, and English, but, of the other languages represented in the collection, I know only some Seraiki. In cases where I had no choice but to work in collaboration with native speakers (often themselves scholars and poets), I decided to use multiple translations of the same poem, often by different hands—a literal, line by line rendition, a plain prose version, and a poetic rendering, with or without the rhyme scheme and meter—to get a better idea of the original. I also advised my collaborators to be absolutely faithful to the imagery of the poems. It helped, of course, that I could read the script and recognize some of the images, expressions, and rhythmic patterns even in languages that I did not know. The receipt of various draft versions was followed by e-mail exchanges and, in many instances, telephone conversations, in which the meanings and connotations of words, images, and metaphors were discussed, often at considerable length.

In happy instances where translators of the sort I was looking for were found, I shared with them the following guidelines to ensure that the anthology would reflect a uniformity of approach:

> 1. Try, as far as possible, to follow the lineation of the original. *Ghazal* couplets are sometimes represented in quatrains in translation, and this is all right, but a certain consistency of approach, a recognizable strategy, in terms of lineation would be certainly helpful;

> 2. It would be helpful if the metaphors and images of the original are faithfully reproduced in translation—again, as far as that is possible— for it is these metaphors and images that may be distinctive in terms of language and cultural tradition. Sometimes this would not be possible—both for obvious and not so obvious reasons—awkwardness of transferred metaphor or image as signifier in the language/culture of translation, culture-specific allusive field, etc. But it is a reasonable goal to keep in mind, perhaps for the very reasons which would render it "strange" or "unfamiliar" or "difficult" in translation;

3. Maintain the micro-formal structures—construction of ideas, vehicles of expression, idiomatic expressions, modes of formulation of ideas (rhetorical questions, plain statements, passive voice, gender ambiguity or specificity, etc.)—as far as possible. The macro or the "framing" form may be the more difficult to transfer into the translated version, especially since there may be far fewer possibilities of rhyming in English than in Urdu (and other subcontinental languages)—and ignoring this may not be a catastrophe—but the micro-structures as building blocks of the original poem should be followed closely as a rule unless there is some overriding and compelling reason not to do so;

4. It follows from this that rhyme may be less important than rhythm in this exercise. If the rhythm or "flow" the poem creates in your head is captured, that would be a major achievement, for the more subtle musicality of the language may be traced in this as opposed to the overt rhyme scheme—again, as a general rule;

5. No explaining should be part of the translations—the connotative field and the allusive environment should, as in the original (and with the originally intended readership) emerge through suggestion. If explanations of peculiar images, ideas, or allusions are needed, they should be relegated to footnotes, if at all;

6. Trust your instinct for the original language of the poem.

It is true that some poems translate better than others, but there are issues relating to grammar and the formulation of ideas, as well as conventions of drawing images and metaphors, on the one hand, and rituals of imparting feelings, emotions, and sensations, on the other, that may be difficult to get across from one language to another. Within the literary tradition of the language of composition, such conventions all have their place; they command instinctive recognition and trigger a frisson of response. In translation, however, they may come across as stylized and mechanistic, or unusual and unfamiliar.

In the poetry of most of the languages from which translations are included here, the line is frequently a unit of meaning, as opposed to sentences that extend over several lines, and this is why it often makes sense to preserve the lineation. There are, however, occasionally quite elaborate syntactical structures, and, because the standard word order in these languages differs from that in English, there were times when following the original lineation would unduly dislocate English syntax. In such cases, it was sometimes necessary to rearrange words across lines, with the goal, nevertheless, of conveying the sequence and timing of expressed thought and feeling as closely as possible without doing violence to English idiom. Even at a very basic level, the subject-verb-object structure natural to English is simply not the standard grammatical sequence in Urdu or in the other languages from which the poems included in this volume are drawn. For example, the opening line of Ahmad Faraz's poem "Mahasara" ("Siege") is "meray ghanim nain mujh ko yeh paigham bheja hae" ("My enemy has sent me this message"), which translates literally as, "My enemy has me to this message sent have." So it can be seen how the conveyance of thought, emotion, or idea in exactly the manner, sequence, and pacing of the original is virtually impossible.

Moreover, the languages represented in this volume use the passive voice far more frequently, and naturally, than is considered appropriate in English. As a general rule, the passive voice was retained when it seemed crucial to the emotional and psychological temper of a line or poem, and it was discarded when it created an awkwardness that clouded the experience of the poem. Punctuation and capitalization present yet another source of anxiety for the translator. In all the original languages of composition represented here, there are no markers for capitalization, and punctuation is minimal. In the rare instances where punctuation does exist, it is hardly standardized or used with any regularity. Invariably, lines do not end with any form of punctuation (even where one would expect a period, a comma, or some other form of punctuation in English). Readers of Urdu, Sindhi, Pashto, Punjabi, Balochi, Seraiki, and Kashmiri are of course accustomed to this convention, and their aesthetic experience and enjoyment of their poetry is partly constituted by this open-ended quality of the line. As an aesthetically significant feature of the poems from these languages, this convention has been largely retained in the translations.

It is well recognized that ideas and images that carry an emotional or intellectual charge in one language may not have the same in another and may appear flat or even wholly obscure outside their linguistic code and context. Thus *gul-o-bulbul* ("the rose and the nightingale"), *maqtal* or the plural *qatal gahain* ("field of execution" or "killing fields"), Karbala (the place of Hazrat Imam Husain's martyrdom), folk characters like Heer, Ranjha, Kaido, Sassi, Punnu, Laila, Majnun, Sohni, Mahiwal, and others, may mean very little to a Western audience, even though these names and terms have a wide circulation in South Asia and parts of the Middle East. The connotations they carry for local readers and audiences cannot be transferred to English, and yet explanations would only have shackled the poetry with academic fetters. I have accordingly kept explanatory notes to a bare minimum. Information about the folk characters, historical allusions, cultural images, and traditional metaphors is readily available on the Internet and from other scholarly sources. For readers to encounter unfamiliar names or terms in a poem and be moved to find out more about them on their own may actually bring the originary experience of the poem closer, make it more personal and intimate.

Yet it is important to keep in mind that for the Muslim poets of the Indo-Pakistan subcontinent in particular, no matter what subcontinental language they use to compose their poems, Persian poetry and its conventions are very often the source of inspiration and emulation. It may be, therefore, instructive to review Wheeler M. Thackston's compact, but thoroughly informative, introduction to his anthology *A Millennium of Classical Persian Poetry*, to get a sense of the energizing aesthetics behind much of the poetry included in this volume. I quote the following passages for their particular relevance in this regard:

> Because poets were expected . . . to have read practically the entire corpus of Persian poetry before they composed their first poem, and because refinement of existing conventions was valued, not innovation, the tradition is cumulative and builds upon itself. The stereotypes of lover and beloved—miserable, suffering, unrequited lover,

and inapproachable beloved—and the *topoi*, the conventional metaphors, that typify these relationships, such as the moth and the candle, the nightingale and the rose, Farhad and Shîrîn, and so forth, all are immutably fixed in the tradition.

The metaphorical language of poetry also developed within the cumulative tradition. What began as a simile, lips red as rubies, for instance, became so commonplace and hackneyed after thousands of repetitions over the decades and centuries that in the end the simile was scrapped, and ruby lips became simply rubies. So also tears that initially rolled down the cheeks like pearls became, in the end, simply pearls, while tears that glistened like stars became stars. A face as round and lovely as the moon similarly became simply the moon. In the twelfth century Nîzamî could write that Lyali's mother . . . bound a necklace of stars onto the moon . . . and know that his audience would immediately understand by this that she covered her daughter's face with tears. (Thackston x)

Some of these and similarly developed conventions have continued to appear in the poetry of subcontinental Muslim poets. The word "shehr" (literally, city) is one such example of a metaphor that has become a convention for referring to the State or country as a whole. It signified initially the metropolis, the capital city of the Caliphate, itself seen as the source of excessive power, false morality, oppressive legislation, and injustice. In time, the imagery describing the metropolis—its surrounding walls, the censorious Magistrate, the tyrannical King residing in safe luxury behind the walls of his formidable fortress, the mercenary guards armed with bows and arrows to defend the King's interests or persecute his enemies, the corrupt state functionaries, the hypocritical religious leaders, the suffocating sense of oppression, the harried and harassed common people—has been transplanted to the modern state to represent its milieu of constraint and duress, persecution, deception, and terror.

Another complicating factor is the mystical strain that runs through the imagery of a good number of poems included here. The overt image itself, like the "beloved" (gender unspecified), the "cup-bearer," "sparrows," "flame" or "lamp," can certainly be read literally, but the poet is almost always working within a tradition where these images have mystical connotations. To be able to pick this out requires some experience with reading poetic texts from the Islamic world or the subcontinental Muslim tradition, and this feature too is the gift of Persian poetic convention and practice. Thackston, again, points out that, for a new reader of Persian poetry (and one may just as well read "subcontinental Muslim poetry" here), the pervasiveness of mysticism in it poses a considerable difficulty:

> Fairly early in the game the mystics found that they could "express the ineffable" in poetry much better than in prose. Usurping the whole of the poetic vocabulary that had been built up by that time, they imbued every word with mystical signification. What had begun as liquid wine with alcoholic content became the "wine of union with the godhead" on which the mystic is "eternally drunk." Beautiful young cupbearers with whom one might like to dally became *sha-hids*, "bearers of witness" to the dazzling beauty of that-which-truly-exists. After the mystics had wrought their influence on the tradition, every word of the poetic vocabulary had acquired such "clouds" of associated meaning from lyricism and mysticism that the two strains merged into one. (Thackston xi)

Thackston goes on to describe how the "Turk" came to represent the beloved and the mole on the beloved's cheek to be described as a "Hindu mole" because of its dark color. Readers of this book will see that many of these images that Thackston discusses are present in the poems of this volume where they have the same or closely similar connotations that are identified here. This is a fascinating subject in itself, but the scope of the introduction does not allow for much further elaboration than has been provided here.

There are certain themes like tribal or ethnic pride, celebration of military glory, fascination with the soldierly life, nationalism, as well as the pleasure (felt by men as well as women) of embracing and reveling in traditional gender roles, that may not travel very well across the linguistic and cultural divide that separates the languages represented here and English. Such feelings are, nonetheless, part of the literary landscape of any language and culture, though their mode of articulation and expression may be different. But there is much else here as well that is likely to strike a chord with American and English-speaking Western readers—challenges to social conventions, critiques of gender inequity, social and political engagement, yearning for a people's revolution, protest against tyranny in all its forms, the need to claim a place for the individual in a society where individuals have become anonymous or absorbed in the abstract collective, philosophical reflections on the self and its relation to the universe, the depths of personal isolation and grief, the allure and the vagaries of love. This anthology spans an enormous range of subject matter and experience. My hope is that the translated poems will read as poems in the language of translation—that they will come across as poems in English, but not as "English poems," that these translations retain the cultural flavors of the original and are successful in passing them on to the readers.

Finally, a brief note on the dominant poetic forms in subcontinental Muslim linguistic and literary cultures may be helpful in understanding the aesthetic dynamics of the works represented in this anthology. To begin with, *ghazal* and *nazm* are the two broad divisions of classical Urdu poetry, *ghazal* being, traditionally, the more popular of the two. This distinction is preserved in other Pakistani language traditions as well. A *ghazal* is composed of a series of couplets, generally between five and twelve, with a rhyme scheme of AA, BA, CA, DA, and so on. The rhyme scheme has two parts, *qafia* and *radif*, which may be translated as rhyme and end rhyme (or rhyme phrase). Both are maintained strictly throughout the *ghazal*. It is important to note that every couplet is autonomous in a *ghazal* and constitutes a theme in itself that sometimes may, but generally is not, continued in the following couplets. This allows the poet considerable freedom, and there are instances where the person being addressed may not be the same throughout the poem. Even the mood may change dramatically from couplet to couplet. The *ghazal*, then, is distinguished by the disunity of its content, a feature that Western readers find disorienting unless they are aware of it as a convention integral to the form. What provides unity to the *ghazal* is its form, i.e., the meter and the rhyming pattern, its *qafia* and *radif*.

A *nazm* is a rhymed poem of any length and follows a strict meter. It has a definite rhyme scheme, though usually more varied than the repetitive double rhyming structure of the *ghazal*. A *nazm* may be lyrical, narrative, or dramatic, but unlike the *ghazal*, it does have unity of theme and content. A *nazm* that does not follow a strict meter nor rely on rhyme—or contain a regular rhyme scheme—is known as *azad nazm*, akin to free verse in English.

Other forms of poetry prevalent in the Arabic and Indo-Iranian traditions that are reflected in Pakistani linguistic and literary cultures include *kafi* (a short devotional poem), *qita* (a short poem within or independent of a *ghazal*), *rubai* (an independent poem of four lines, a quatrain), *qawwali* (based on *qaul,* a famous saying, generally from Hadith, having its origin in ninth century Baghdad—*qawwals* are those who recite the *qauls*), *qasida* (a eulogy or panegyric in rhymed couplets), *sufi* (also known as *sufiana kalam*— literally, mystical speech), *marsiya* (elegy, generally in commemoration of Imam Husain's martyrdom at Karbala), and the *masnavi* (a narrative poem in rhymed couplets). Those peculiar to the Indo-Iranian culture include *bol* (sayings, proverbs), *doha* (rhymed couplets), *geet* (song of love, devotion, or pain of separation), *thumri* (a semiclassical song genre in the woman's voice), though *ghazal, nazm, qawwali,* and *sufiana kalam* are all extremely popular in Pakistan. It is also significant that the gender of the poetic persona and the addressee in many of these forms may often be indeterminate or may be any one of the following pairings: male to male, female to male, male to female, and female to female.

In conclusion, I would like to acknowledge here the debt I owe to the many wonderful translators, literary critics, and commentators whose work has given me such enjoyment over the years and from whom I have learned much to help me shape my own views about translating poetry. I am also grateful for the support of my department faculty at Agnes Scott College. Their generosity of spirit has redefined for me the inestimable worth of cherished colleagues. Nor could this work have been accomplished without the patience, flexibility, and understanding with which Ivar Nelson, former director of Eastern Washington University Press, helped me negotiate my way. His encouragement kept me going even when my spirit flagged sometimes. Christopher Howell, senior editor at the Press and himself a poet, provided a gifted second sight. His suggestions were always helpful, often more widely than the context in which they were made. That said, it was Pamela Holway, managing editor of Eastern Washington Press, whose rigorous scrutiny of the translations and meticulous editorial comments, questions, and suggestions helped guide this work to its present form. My deepest thanks to her for the professional excellence she brought to her work. She has been an inspiration in many ways. I also wish to thank Dalkey Archive Press for bringing this labor to publication.

I would be seriously remiss if I did not mention the patience and self-denial of my family during the time I worked on this anthology. As always, it was the love and care of my wife, Maryam, that sustained me throughout. I only hope that what I have to offer here is not entirely unworthy of all the goodwill, affection, and accommodation extended to me by friends, colleagues, and family alike.

WAQAS KHWAJA

BIBLIOGRAPHY

Bahu, Sultan. *Death Before Dying: The Sufi Poems of Sultan Bahu.* Translated by Jamal Elias. Berkeley: University of California Press, 1998.

Barnstone, Tony. "The Poem Behind the Poem: Literary Translation as American Poetry." In *The Poem Behind the Poem: Translating Asian Poetry*, edited by Frank Stewart, 1–16. Port Townsend, WA: Copper Canyon Press, 2004.

Barnstone, Willis. "How I Strayed into Asian Poetry." In *The Poem Behind the Poem: Translating Asian Poetry*, edited by Frank Stewart, 28–38. Port Townsend, WA: Copper Canyon Press, 2004.

Faiz, Ahmed Faiz. *The Rebel's Silhouette: Selected Poems.* Translated by Agha Shahid Ali. Amherst: University of Massachusetts Press, 1991.

—. *The True Subject: Selected Poems of Faiz Ahmad Faiz.* Translated by Naomi Lazard. Lahore: Vanguard Books, 1988.

Frank, Bernhard, trans. *Modern Hebrew Poetry.* Iowa City: University of Iowa Press, 1980.

Franklin, Michael J. "Accessing India: Orientalism, Anti-'Indianism,' and the Rhetoric of Jones and Burke." In *Romanticism and Colonialism: Writing and Empire, 1780–1830*, edited by Tim Fulford and Peter J. Kitson, 48–66. Cambridge: Cambridge University Press, 2005.

Fulford, Tim, and Peter J. Kitson, eds. *Romanticism and Colonialism: Writing and Empire, 1780–1830.* Cambridge: Cambridge University Press, 2005.

Ghalib, Mirza. *The Seeing Eye: Selections from the Urdu and Persian Ghazals of Ghalib.* Translated by Ralph Russell. Islamabad, Pakistan: Alhamra Publishers, 2003.

Grosjean, Ok-Koo Kang. "The Way of Translation." In *The Poem Behind the Poem: Translating Asian Poetry*, edited by Frank Stewart, 62–75. Port Townsend, WA: Copper Canyon Press, 2004.

Habib, M.A.R., ed. and trans. *An Anthology of Modern Urdu Poetry, in English Translation with Urdu Text.* New York: Modern Language Association of America, 2003.

Iqbal, Allama Muhammad. *Poems from Iqbal: Renderings in English Verse with Comparative Urdu Text.* Translated by Victor Kiernan. Karachi: Oxford University Press, 2004.

Jamal, Mahmood, ed. *The Penguin Book of Modern Urdu Poetry.* New York: Penguin, 1986.

Jones, Sir William. *Poems, Consisting Chiefly of Translations from the Asiatick Languages, to Which Are Added Two Essays: I. On the Poetry of the Eastern Nations; II. On the Arts, Commonly Called Imitative.* Second edition. London: W. Bowyer and J. Nichols for N. Conant, 1777 [1772].

Merwin, W. S. "Preface to *East Window: The Asian Translations.*" In *The Poem Behind the Poem: Translating Asian Poetry*, edited by Frank Stewart, 152–62. Port Townsend, WA: Copper Canyon Press, 2004.

Pritchett, Frances W. *Nets of Awareness: Urdu Poetry and Its Critics.* Berkeley and Los Angeles: University of California Press, 1994.

—. "Personal Website at Columbia University." www.columbia.edu/itc/mealac/pritchett/00fwp/

—. "Translation of Iqbal's 'Masjid-e-Qurtubah.'" http://www.columbia.edu/itc/mealac/pritchett/00urdu/iqbal/masjid_index.html

Sorley, H. T. *Shah Abdul Latif of Bhit: His Poetry, Life and Times; A Study of Literary, Social and Economic Conditions in Eighteenth Century Sind.* New Delhi: Ashish Publishing House, 1984.

Stewart, Frank, ed. *The Poem Behind the Poem: Translating Asian Poetry.* Port Townsend, WA: Copper Canyon Press, 2004.

Syed, Najm Hosain. *Recurrent Patterns in Punjabi Poetry.* Lahore: Majlis Shah Husain, 1968.

Thackston, Wheeler M. *A Millennium of Classical Persian Poetry: A Guide to the Reading and Understanding of Persian Poetry from the Tenth to the Twentieth Century.* Bethesda, Maryland: Ibex Publishers, 2000.

MODERN POETRY OF PAKISTAN

ALLAMA MUHAMMAD IQBAL

The Great Mosque of Córdoba

I

Succession of day and night
shaper of occurrences
Succession of day and night
origin of life and death

Succession of day and night
a double-colored silk thread
From which the self weaves
a garment of its attributes

Succession of day and night
lament of eternity's lute strings
Through which the self discovers
the register of possibility

It examines you
it examines me
Succession of day and night
appraiser of all created worlds

If you fall short
if I fall short
Death is your reward
death is my reward

What is the truth
of your days and nights?
A torrent of passing time
in which there is no day, no night

The miracles of ingenuity
are all transient and fleeting
The world's affairs are impermanent
the world's affairs are impermanent

The beginning and end, extinction
the hidden and manifest, extinction
Ancient image or new
its journey's end, extinction

II

But in that image there is
the coloring of permanence
Which may have been by
some man-of-God secured

The man-of-God's work
is illuminated by love
Love is the root of life
death is forbidden to it

Though time's tidal flow
is furious and swift
Love itself is a flood
that holds back its swell

In love's almanac
besides the present age
Are other epochs as well
that have no name

Love, the breath of Jibraeel
love, the heart of Mustafa
Love, God's Messenger
love, the word of God

With love's ecstasy is
the rose's face radiant
Love is wine in fermentation
love, the cup that overflows

Love, the Sanctuary's lawgiver
love, the commander of troops
Love is born of the journey
it has a thousand stages

From love's plectrum arises
the song of the string of life
Love is the light of life
love is the fire of life

III

O mosque of Córdoba
you spring from love
Love entirely imperishable
exempt from inconstancy

It may be paint, or stone and brick
a lute, or word and voice
The miracle of art has
its birth from the heart's blood

A drop of blood from the heart
turns stone into a beating heart
The cry from the heart's blood
fire, exhilaration, and song

Your atmosphere delights the heart
my song inflames the breast
From you, the spectacle of hearts
from me, the burgeoning of hearts

No less than the highest heaven
lies within man's breast
Although for man's fistful of dust
the blue sky is the utmost limit

What matters if the act of prostration
is available to the being of light?
Not within its reach is
the fire and fervor of submission

I am a Hindi infidel
look at my zeal and devotion
Prayer and benediction in my heart
prayer and benediction on my lips

There is yearning in my melody
there is yearning in my pipe

The song of "Allah Hu"
rings in my flesh and bones

IV

Your elegance and your majesty
are evidence of the man-of-God
He is grand and glorious
you, too, are grand and glorious

Your foundation secure
your columns, innumerable
Like a grove of date palms
In Syrian sands

On your doors and rooftops
the vale of Yemen's light
Your tall minarets
the stage for Jibraeel's display

Never can he perish
the man-of-Islam, since
His calls to prayer proclaim
the secret of Moses and Abraham

His land, limitless
his horizon, boundless
The Tigris, Danube, and Nile
are but a wave in his ocean

Strange and wondrous his worlds
his fables, marvelous
He gave to the old order
the signal for departure

Cupbearer to learned men of taste
a rider in the field of yearning
His wine is pure
his sword noble

He is a true soldier
his armor, faith, *La ila*
Beneath the nurture of the sword
his iteration *La ila*

V

Through you became evident
the mystery of the man-of-faith
The heat of his days
the tenderness of his nights

His high station
his noble imagination
His rapture, his eagerness
his humility, his pride

The hand of Allah
is the believing man's hand
Triumphant and ingenious
resolver of difficulties, skilled

His nature a mix of dust and light
man, with divine attributes
More generous than the two worlds
is his selfless heart

His hopes modest
his objectives eminent
His manner captivating
his glance soothing

Gentle in conversation
fervent in seeking
In battle or social company
pure of heart, pure of deed

The center of Truth's compass
is the faith of the man-of-God
And this whole world
fancy, a magic spell, a trope

He is the destination of wisdom
the distillation of love
In the fraternity of worlds
he is the life of the gathering

VI

Mecca of the accomplished
glory of manifest faith
Through you is sanctified
the land of Andalusians

If beneath the heavens there is
a peer to your beauty
It is within a Mussalman's heart
and nowhere else

Ah! Those men of righteousness
those Arabian horsemen
Forebears of a great people
owners of truth and conviction

Through whose governance
this strange mystery is unveiled
That the empire of the brave
is abstinence, not regal writ

Whose visions
instructed East and West
Whose intellect lit up a trail
in the night of Europe

Because of the gift of whose blood
to this day Andalusians are
Cheerful and passionate
candid-browed and fair

Even today in this land
the gazelle-eye is common
And the darts of loving glances
are still pleasing to the heart

The scent of Yemen even now
hangs in its air

The manner of the Hejaz still
imbues its songs

VII

In the eye of the star
your earth is the exalted sky
Alas, for centuries
your air has heard no call to prayer

In which valley
at what stage of the journey
Is the hardy caravan
of awe-inspiring love today?

Germany has already seen
the tumult of the Reformation
Which has not spared anywhere
traces of antiquated forms

The Pope's prestige
lost its sanctity
And the frail boat of reason
was set in motion

The French eye, too
has witnessed a revolution
That altered the complexion
of the Western world

The nation descended of Rome
old in its worship of the past
Taking pleasure in renewal
it, too, is young once more

In the Mussalman's soul
there is today the same ferment
This is God's secret
not for the tongue to utter it

Let us see, from this ocean's
depth, what wonder springs
What colors
the blue dome takes

VIII

In the mountain's valley
clouds are sunk in evening light
Heaps of Badakhshan jewels
the sun has left behind

Simple and passionate
is the peasant girl's song
For the heart's boat
the time of youth is turbulent

O moving waters of Guadalquivir
someone by your shore
Sees today
a dream of another age

The new world is as yet
behind the veil of destiny
In my eyes, however
its dawn has been unveiled

If I lift the curtain
from the face of my reflections
Europe will not withstand
the radiance of their splendor

Where there is no revolution
that life is death
The spirit of a nation
the striving for revolution

Like a sword in the hand of fate
is the nation that
In every age maintains
a reckoning of its deeds

All pictures are incomplete
without the heart's blood
Song is puerile frenzy
without the heart's blood

Translated from Urdu by Waqas Khwaja

JOSH MALIHABADI

Address

I

With what face, traders, do you propose
to uphold human goodness in the world today?

"The one they call Hitler is a wolf, a wolf!
Shoot down the wolf, for peace, for survival.

An autumn gale threatens the world's garden,
humanity is reduced to sobs and sighs.

Hitler's hand commands the steed of arrogance—
Quell Germany's fire with the shower of swords."

II

I am surprised. Such conversation—in your councils?
Now you fret over the fate of the species?

When you first arrived to trade in this land,
were you not already familiar with such a notion?

Was the spirit of freedom lacking in the people of Hind?
Be honest! Were they not a society of human beings?

III

Don't you remember the chronicle of your own misdeeds?
Recall the Company's rule of lawlessness?

When you ranged across the country plundering caravan after caravan,
reduced the flower of Hind's pride to vagrants in their own land?

When you went around splitting the thumbs of weavers and craftsmen,
and filled up the moats with cold, dead bodies?

A deathlike pall spread over Hindustan's industry,
a calamity worked by your hands.

IV

But, by God, how you hanker after justice today!
By Mir Jafar's head—was Siraj an enemy of truth?

Have you forgotten your assault on the begums of Avadh,
and the days of the Rani of Jhansi's resistance?

Do you recall the scene of Bahadur Shah's exile,
and lion-hearted Tipu's calamitous tale?

To succor him when he sagged under three days of starvation,
whose heads did you present to the Emperor Zafar?

You will remember too the history of Mitya Burj,
from whose earth black fumes arise to this day?

You must often have visited Qaisar Bagh as well,
where the cry of "Ah, Akhtar!" can be heard still.

Say, truly, do you have no memory of that outrageous injustice,
whose witness to this day is a grave in Rangoon?

More recent injury to Hindis must be fresh in your mind
    too—
I am sure you remember the Jallianwala Bagh massacre too?

Go, ask him why his name is so illustrious.
That wolf-faced Dyer is living still!

And Bhagat Singh, for whom even today the heart mourns—
do you remember the noose that you placed round his neck?

In what conditions were Hind's guides and guardians forced to
    dwell?
Put this question to prison doors and walls,

where imperial arrogance is still preserved,
where the sound of the whip's lash echoes still.

V

Why do you now sail your ship on the passions of the masses?
I am much surprised you preach lessons today of fairness.

The powerful are never caught in the trap of equity,
they never show much concern for the rights of humanity.

VI

But today you advise about morals and courtesy:
I suspect you don't feel as mighty as once you did.

Those who uphold what is right are civilized, the mischief-makers,
    savage—
these are really the principles of weak nations.

Is it perhaps that today you no longer command centers of power—
for why not still claim that he who wields the stick takes the buffalo?

What did you say—that mankind's first duty is justice?
Have you no longer the strength to murder and persecute?

VII

You linger too long beneath the date palm of integrity.
God forbid! I hope you haven't sprained an ankle!

The sound of hooves is heard in neither city nor wilderness.
Is all well, or is the stallion of war in the infirmary?

Today, every eye is suffused with compassion.
Are you (may this be your enemy's fate!) suffering some illness?

Just a little winded, and you are in love with justice—
and want fresh air for the entire human race?

Forgetting how you persecuted, you now sing of fairness.
Is there a fire in your home that you raise this alarm?

It doesn't behoove a felon to make such a din—
Yazid and Shimr until yesterday, today you pretend to be Husain!

Your safety, bargain hunters, now lies only in this:
bend your neck low before time's decree.

Now time will write a story with a new theme,
and its title requires the ink of your blood.

The decree of time cannot be deflected.
Death can be averted, but not time's decree.

Translated from Urdu by Khurram Khurshid and Waqas Khwaja

O stranger, if you wish to seek Josh,
he will be in the circle of the wise before dawn.

In the morning this lover of nature's sights
will be near a garden or a patch of wilderness,

and during the day, in search of secrets and precise sense,
in the city of artists and the writers' retreat.

In the evening this man of God, reprobate of the tavern,
can be found in the vintner's hallowed house of blessings.

At night, a friend of flowing curls and fair faces,
find him rapt with song and dance or in his beloved's street.

And if there is news of oppression somewhere, this poor fellow
like a corpse will be prone in the house of grief.

Translated from Urdu by Khurram Khurshid and Waqas Khwaja

HAFEEZ JALANDHARI

Staff of Old Age

Fled, that time of self-indulgence,
the world of noise and uproar, wrecked.
Autumn has despoiled
the playful wantonness, the air's ecstasy.
The caravan of life has passed
beyond youth's valley of joy.
Annihilation's pathway of terrors beckons,
towering cliffs on one side, chasms on the other.
Fled, that time of self-indulgence.

The journey, and night's darkness,
with no sense of dawning day—
to stop and start again, it cannot be.
Life's effects packed and ready to go,
no provisions for the journey among them,
and a brigand awaits to seize the breath.
The self-serving my only companions,
no one devoted to you or me.
The journey, and night's darkness.

A thousand obstacles at every step,
neither love's company nor reason's counsel.
It is hard to keep a steady step,
for the feet find no footing on the ground.
A slight slip,
and the skull will shatter.
Such are the perils of the road—

and then this keen and cutting wind.
A thousand obstacles at every step.

Bereft of understanding,
the senses, too, have dulled,
but travelers keep going,
for now there is no escape.
On the forehead of hope's firmament
just one star, alone, shines—
that my young one accompanies me,
the staff of my old age.
This, the only star that shines.

Translated from Urdu by Khurram Khurshid and Waqas Khwaja

What Am I?

These great thoughts!
What am I?
In the river's midst,
an orphan.
A lonesome anguish,
a hot teardrop,
a cold sigh.
In the deep and turbulent sea of human blood,
in catastrophes, in earthquakes,
in lightning and in thunder,
a voice without a voice.
No one listens.
O God, my benevolent sustainer!
what is this hope and fear?
These great thoughts!
What am I?

Translated from Urdu by Khurram Khurshid and Waqas Khwaja

Yearning for Free Time

This is how time passes,
yearning for leisure,
like some leaf
floating downriver
drifting to the edge
wishing to linger
and ramble through
the reflection of trees
that adorns
the river's surface;
or a waft of memory
accustomed to the flow
desires to rest
in a garden nook
and fill its lap
with the fragrance of a flower
that is yet to bloom.

Yearning for leisure,
this is how time passes.
Worries about a livelihood
leave no spare time whatever.
I wish with all my heart
to acquire a skill,
to fill the arms of art
with the roses of my themes.
But my luck is out—

I simply don't have time.
Where would I find the leisure?
Time is the problem.

Then it strikes me, perhaps luxury is not out of reach.
I should think of doing something
that would bring in a lot of money.
But, then again, I reason,
this business of thinking
can be conducted only if I have the time.
They just don't leave me any free time,
worries of subsistence!

Translated from Urdu by Khurram Khurshid and Waqas Khwaja

Come to Salvation

Rise, O selfish Pukhtuns!
if you wish to be rid of troubles.

Lift your heads to know life!
Life lies in action and movement.

Rise with dagger, spear, and flag—
rise as thunder, squall, and soothing breeze!

Hold back your pride and power,
tend the painful heart of the world.

Rouse the sleeping ones with the cry of Takbir.
The awakened drift back to sleep—rouse them again!

Don't you see that people have gone astray?
That human values, at every moment, are in decline?

The community of Abraham discordant and divided—
unthinkable once, this has become reality today.

Follow the right path, day and night—
be the caravan's guide, its eyes and feet.

Listen! Right is right, but might is right as well.
This is the lesson time has taught me.

O Pukhtuns, listen to me, and reflect!
O brave ones, listen to me, and reflect!

That I weep and wail day and night—
understand what I want, what I say!

I am not in need of food, I am not poor.
I pray for your peace, for your prosperity.

I want the Pukhtun forever on the move,
the Qur'an in one hand, the sword in the other.

Who is proud to be part of the best of nations?
To crush those who lay waste the beautiful garden?

Who walks through the perils of fire?
Who offers life for truth and justice?

I want the Pukhtun to be vital and alive,
his inner being resting in his heart like a pearl.

A Pukhtun's tribe and lineage are of no concern to me—
I want to see the Pukhtun united as a nation.

I see the nation and community in disarray,
but I want the true Pukhtun, the bold and honored Pukhtun.

What comparison between one who fights for gold and land
and Bilal, who fought for honor, obedient to God?

O Pukhtun! That is how I want to see you.
Even such a Majnun as he was, my dear,

who sacrificed his life and wealth for love,
for such is the promise of Paradise from God.

The promise of God is firm, but based on just deserts—
be like Salman, Abuzar, or Bilal!

Your destination is far, your journey long:
it means submission, compliance, guidance, and nurturing.

Sacrificing life and wealth is the mark of generosity—
the holy warrior and the martyr gain in either case.

He is not a Pukhtun who kills his cousin.
The good Pukhtun earns the mercy of divine light in a just war.

It is dogs who fight for meat and selfish gain:
the true fight is fought in the way of God.

The true fight is fought for a just cause,
true honor shown in striving for the Lord.

Pukhtuns are never the aggressors but stout in defense,
never pursue land or wealth that is not theirs.

Combine faith and Pukhto, and you are a true Pukhtun.
Otherwise, a blot of shame on life.

If you sweat and shed blood for Pukhto,
the Pukhto of God will be revealed to you.

God is Pukhtun and favors the Pukhtun.
He defends the Pukhtun and contends on his behalf.

Translated from Pashto by Sher Zaman Taizi and Pervez Sheikh

Ghazal: Is It a Glittering Gem That Hangs from Your Ear, Love?

Is it a glittering gem that hangs from your ear, love?
Or morning dew on a flower-leaf quivering?

You call me mad, but it's you who are deluded.
Simpleton! Madness is the lover's virtue.

I assemble my shattered heart, but it falls again to pieces.
How strangely the memory of your flowing hair affects me!

Nine and twenty times I have struck my head along the way.
And every time I thought it was your door.

It's all within me, this contest of joy and grief.
Else the world is neither Paradise nor Hell.

On a worthless head the turban is like a mushroom in the desert.
Not every turban is a turban, nor every head worthy of it.

The bright-faced came to bid me farewell!
O Samandar, you should be happy to embark on your journey.

Translated from Pashto by Sher Zaman Taizi and Pervez Sheikh

Ghazal: None Has Such Bewitching Eyes

None has such bewitching eyes,
eyes lively, yet bashful.

I would offer my head for those eyes
that sparkle every morning in the sky.

Fools call them heavy with sleep,
but these are eyes that revive the dying.

A hundred hearts they peg with their lances.
Take care! These black eyes are full of mischief.

Come soothe and dress the wounds of my eyes—
I have waited for you a long time.

The home of my heart lies in ruins.
Who plotted? Who laid it waste? It was your eyes.

O Marghalaray! My pearl! My life for a glimpse of you!
But the eyes of Kashmala are something else again.

They promise but have no power of speech—
O my love, your eyes are without the means to speak.

How can he conceal his feelings from the world?
The eyes of Samandar well up perpetually.

Translated from Pashto by Sher Zaman Taizi and Pervez Sheikh

AMIR HAMZA KHAN SHINWARI

Ghazal: I Learned to Bow When I Lost My Head

I learned to bow when I lost my head.
Love saw failure of prudence, with all hope gone.

My hidden faults surfaced in the light of your love.
Motes are not visible without the sun.

You came in the night, left in the night, and it is still night.
I did not realize this night had no end.

Nothing but a mocking smile for me?
My tears have made no impression on you.

My desire for you thrust me before the dog.
I thought no warden stood guard at your door.

Your cheeks glowed at the sight of my portrait—
Whoever said the blind cannot see!

Two eyes, he said, together see one object,
Is it Hamza's double vision or your duplicity?

Translated from Pashto by Sher Zaman Taizi and Pervez Sheikh

Ghazal: I Seek a Simple Definition of Fate

I seek a simple definition of fate:
the mirror of artifice I seek.

I seek neither fate nor artifice,
but knowledge of love and beauty I seek.

The languorous stretching of my lover at dawn—
for a lifetime of sleepless nights I seek.

For me the calamity of her coiling hair.
Mad that I am, these binding chains I seek.

I dreamed both worlds were but an illusion.
An interpretation of this dream I seek.

I am weary of this utter silence—
your picture to converse with I seek.

One who will instruct me in the mysteries of the self,
O love, in you such a guide I seek.

Fair faces no longer interest my eyes:
in all I see, your peer I seek.

I questioned her about the breaking of hearts.
You weep, she said, to repair the heart I seek.

Today, unexpectedly, you asked how I was.
Some time to compose my answer I seek.

What matter, if I vanquish your world?
To conquer my own world I seek.

I peer through your hair to glimpse your face:
the state of Kashmir from the Hindu I seek!

O Hamza! Your words may be eloquent indeed,
the fulfillment of intention is what I seek.

Translated from Pashto by Pervez Sheikh

Ghazal: I Shall Always Go with the Brave Pukhtun

I shall always go with the brave Pukhtun—
a Pukhtun, I with Pukhto will go.

O nation's sun! Like morning dew,
I with your scorching rays would go.

They who threw caution to the wind for their nation,
I too with the delirious like these would go.

Beware! I am not the evil eye that
with the smoke of wild rue I would go.

Strangers call it the language of Hell—
but to Paradise I with Pukhto would go.

I am not the sun that cannot return,
but with the inclination of the day I go.

The heritage of my past lies still in the east:
I am not the sun that to the west would go.

If the youth bloom into the world of Pukhtun
then I with these brave young spirits would go.

To the future I bring traditions of the past,
to both with the pomp of the present I go.

Unless I bring the Pukhtun together,
with *jirgas* I to every *tapa* would go.

O Hamza! The journey may be to the Hejaz,
but I with the caravan of Pukhtun will go!

Translated from Pashto by Pervez Sheikh

Ghazal: Since I Have Known Your Benevolence

Since I have known your benevolence,
humility has overcome in me both conceit and caprice.

I am revealed to myself gradually,
myself the secret at the heart of the universe.

Beware of those who make eyes at you, my dear.
I too have my eye on them, and you, through the day.

Foolish to worry about sorrows as the end draws near,
since the end was known from the very beginning.

I am neither mortal nor one who returns,
but the sound of an echo that sweeps across the desert.

Good or bad, you made me who I am.
Please tell me, then, where lies my fault?

You remain captive to the twisting curls of your hair.
Hamza, he is miles away from you!

Translated from Pashto by Sher Zaman Taizi and Pervez Sheikh

Ghazal: To Whomever You Belong, I Long for You

To whomever you belong, I long for you.
I praise you because I belong to you.

The light in your enchanting eyes
is a reflection of the way I imagine you.

When you appeared, I forgot what I wanted to say,
but I remember something I had meant to say.

I swear by the strands of your sinuous hair,
I am a fettered slave to you.

I know not what or who I am,
as I stare at the spectacle of the world.

A sardonic smile plays on your lips—
but see, I weep, so it seems to you.

Come, my heart, let's enjoy the world,
the world that inhabits her scornful eye!

Why turn to look at me again and yet again?
To make amends? Go on, rest content—I do not sigh.

That every face looks familiar to me
might be because I am so close to you.

Love finds comfort in discontent and distress.
Like a millstone I go around the same axis.

O Hamza! When I saw your peerless beauty,
I knew in that moment I belonged to you.

Translated from Pashto by Sher Zaman Taizi and Pervez Sheikh

Afraid of Life?

Are you afraid of life?
You are life; I, too, am life.
Are you afraid of man?
You are man; I, too, am man.
Man is language, man is speech.
You are not afraid of man.
To the affinity of word and sense
man is attached.
To the hem of man's garment, life is attached.
You are not afraid of that!
The unsaid, then—are you afraid of it?
The moment that has not yet come, are you afraid of it?
The awareness of its approach, are you afraid of it?

Earlier, too, have passed by
seasons of unworthiness, of God's, and nature's, blamelessness.
Do you then still believe it is worthless to desire,
that this night when the tongue is silenced is God's decree?
But what would you know?
If lips don't move, hands come alive,
hands come alive as a sign along the way,
as a tongue of pure light—
hands break into speech as the morning call for prayer.
Are you afraid of light?
You are light; I, too, am light.
You are afraid of light?

From city walls
the demon's spell that lay on them is cleansed at last,
the robe of night
is split at last, is dust at last.
From the dragon of human multitudes comes a singular cry,
the call of self,
as if on desire's path the traveler's blood leaps,
a new madness springs.
People spill over,
people laugh, look! Cities hum again with life, look!
Is it the present that alarms you?
The "now," yes, which you are too, which I am too?
It is the present that alarms you!

Translated from Urdu by Waqas Khwaja

Death of Israfil

Weep for the death of Israfil.
He, the companion of gods, master of discourse,
immortal soul of the human voice,
boundless song of heavens,
still, today, like an incomplete word.
Weep for the death of Israfil!

Come, let us shed tears at this untimely vision of Israfil
recumbent beside his trumpet,
as if a tempest had tossed him to the shore.
Silent, in gleaming sunlight, on the sandy beach,
he lies asleep beside his horn.
His headdress, his locks, his beard,
how tarnished with dust!
How that trumpet of his, from which once flowed
life and death, lies far from his lips,
lost in its own screams, its wails,
the instrument that once lit up temples and altars.

Weep for Israfil,
a roar embodied, a song incarnate,
a sign of heavenly sounds from eternity to eternity.

At Israfil's death,
row after row of angels mourn,
the son of Adam, head in the dust, wastes away,
God's eyes flow with grief.

Not a sound from the skies,
no trumpet call from the mystic worlds.

With Israfil's death,
the provisions of sound are closed to this world,
provisions for minstrels, for musical instruments.
How will the singer now sing, and what will that song be?
The heartstrings of the listeners, mute!
What moves will a dancer make, what steps rehearse?
The assembly's floor, its walls and doors, mute!
What will the city's preacher say now?
The thresholds of the mosques, their domes and minarets,
    mute!
What snare will the hunter of thought lay?
The birds of brook and mountain, mute!

The death of Israfil is
the death of ears that hear, of lips that speak,
the death of the eye that perceives, the heart that is wise.
Because of him was all the hum and howl of dervishes,
conference between the gentle-hearted—
the gentle-hearted who have this day retired, a note stuck in
    their throats.
Gone now the song of praise, the sacred recitation,
the approach to every street and lane now gone,
this last refuge, gone!

With Israfil's death,
this world's time, it seems, has gone to sleep, has turned to stone,
as if someone had swallowed entire all the sounds.
Such loneliness, not even beauty's perfection haunts the mind—
such silence, one cannot recall even one's own name!

With Israfil's death,
the world's tyrants will be left only to dream
of suppressing speech,
of that sovereign power in which, at least,
whispers of the oppressed can be heard.

Translated from Urdu by Waqas Khwaja

Hassan the Potter

I

Jahanzad, below in the street, before your door
Here I stand, heart on fire, Hassan the potter!
This morning in the market, at old man
Yousuf the perfumer's shop, I saw you,
and in your eyes was that fire
Longing for which I have wandered mad for nine years;
Jahanzad, for nine years I have wandered mad!
Lost in that desire,
I never turned toward my sad pots,
those images of my restless hands
lifeless creations of dust and color and oil,
who now whisper:
"Where is Hassan the potter?
Creating us, he's become a god!"
Jahanzad, nine years passed over me
as time treads over some buried city:
Dust in flowerpots
whose fragrance I would fondly breathe
now laden with stones:
Goblet, enamel, cup, pitcher, lantern, flower-vase
All hope of an art of expressing
my worthless existence
lay dead,
and I, Hassan the potter, dust on my head,
disheveled hair, prostrate on the potter's wheel

like some downcast god
creating pots in a dream world of being and nothing,
saw, in your bright eyes of Caucasus
that fire
through which my body and soul became travelers
through cloud and moonlight.
Jahanzad, that dreamy night in Baghdad,
the bank of the river Tigris,
the ship, the closed eyes of that sailor:
For some weary, grief-laden potter
one night alone was alive,
which even now claims his
spirit, his body;
only one night's joy the river's wave granted
in which Hassan the potter sunk, never to surface.

And now, Jahanzad, each day
that unlucky fortune comes to haunt me,
prostrated on the potter's wheel,
it shakes me by the shoulders
(that wheel which year to year was my only hope of
    livelihood):
"Hassan the potter, come to your senses!
Cast an eye on your desolate house.
How shall these children be fed?
Hassan, love-struck fool!
Leave that sport of the rich
and look to your own house."
In my ear that rebuking voice resounded
as if calling down a whirlpool to a drowning man.
Yes, that lake of tears was a lake of flowers;
but I, Hassan the potter, was enchanted
by ruins of the city of illusions,

with no sound, no motion,
no shadow of a bird in flight,
no trace of life.

Jahanzad, in your street today,
against night's chilling darkness,
I stand restless before your door:
Through the window, those enchanting eyes
gaze at me again.
The age, Jahanzad, is a potter's wheel on which,
like enamel, cup, pitcher,
lantern and flower-vase,
humans are created and destroyed.
I am human, yet
these nine years have passed in the shape of grief:
Hassan the potter is today a heap of dust
without a sign of moisture.
Jahanzad, this morning in the bazaar at
the perfumer Yousuf's shop, your eyes
have spoken once again
breathing moisture into dust:
Perhaps this dust will waken into clay.

Who knows the expanse of desire, Jahanzad, but
if you wish, I'll become once more
that same potter whose pots
were the pride of every palace and quarter, every city and
    village,
brightening the dwellings of both rich and poor.
Who knows the expanse of desire, Jahanzad, but
if you wish, I'll turn once more toward my sad pots,
those dried pans of being and nothing,
toward hope of an art to mirror my livelihood:

From that being and nothing, from that color and oil,
to strike again those sparks by which
the ruins of hearts are illumined.

II

Jahanzad,
how shall I forget
the wayward delight of that one night?
Was it wine or the trembling of my hand
caused a glass to topple and break
you were hardly surprised:
Your glass had suffered cracks before!
Jahanzad,
returning from Baghdad to
these pots, these earthen pans,
I reflect upon how you've been a mirror before me,
in public, at the window, at the head of an ermine bed—
a mirror, where nothing
has surfaced but
my own face,
fear of my own pathetic solitude.
As I write to you,
that mirror and its one face
lie in my hand.
And why should this mirror, my tablet, not be
Etched with tears?

Jahanzad,
will you ever bring to me again
the delights of that wanton night?
Time

is the moth, crawling
on walls, mirrors, cups, glasses,
on my jars, pitchers, and pans.
Like crawling time, perhaps
Hassan the potter will return, his soul burning.

Returning, I wonder
if I'm not the web of the spider deprivation,
being woven on this cottage roof,
this dark cottage where I muse, prostrate.
My poor ancestors
left only one trace.
This is the story of their craft, their livelihood.
Now that I have returned, that luckless fortune
comes to stare at me
and will not cease.
In this my cottage, there's nothing.
A game of simple love
we play
in the growing hollowness of night and day,
crying, singing, laughing
together,
just an excuse to keep the heart alive, no more.
Words have limits, Jahanzad, meaning a limit.
Love, youth, tears and smiles,
All have limits.
(Have then the pain of loss
and isolation no limit, no end?)
In my cottage
many aromas
hover about me,
like the smell of that one night they cling.
What dusty aromas linger here—

aromas of my poverty, loneliness,
memories and desires.
But still in this cottage, dirty, disheveled,
there's nothing,
though sometimes the song of birds drifts from far
    trees,
and fragrance from gardens of olives and figs.
Then I'm cheered
and glad to have bathed and emerged.
Else, in this house, there's no bed, no perfume,
not even a fan.
The love you know so well
is beyond my strength.

You'll laugh, Jahanzad, at my strangeness,
my bounty with emotion,
my worship of things,
my seeking a wealth which is not mine.
You who laughed that night at my vacillation
laugh, laugh again at my divided state!

Yet who from love has found anything beyond self?
Jahanzad, all questions
of love have but one answer:
A lover.
It is enough that the heart's voice should echo.
Jahanzad,
it was the voice in a corner of my heart
echoing
at the shores of my art, frozen in time.
Your eyes were an ocean whose endless gaze
froze those shores in their stilled centuries.
Ocean, mirror of my Self,

of the faces of my pots destroyed and created;
of each art and its worshipper,
the mirror.

III

Jahanzad,
the pool of that tavern at Aleppo, that silence of night
where we swam, embracing,
waves outspreading, circle around circle:
We swam the whole night, holding
each other, body and soul,
swimming with delightful fear,
just as water swims in tears,
content in each other, against the tide of age.
You teased me: "Your longing, Hassan, has
dragged you even here!"
But now a fear swims in my heart,
I left my body in that pool at Aleppo,
yet no dualism haunts me.
Even now, I've faith that body and soul are one,
faith that absorbed
me into self.
Before all else I am "self."
If only we exist, still
I am
self before all things.
How could I betray this?

Women like you,
complex beyond
Unraveling,

no one has been able to understand.
To say I had unveiled your depth
would be self-deceit.
The fabric of Woman is self-satire
for which we are no answer

(Who is Labib? Words of whom all night
stole from your lips,
who was it kept pulling at your hair,
tearing at your lips,
as I never could?
Yes, whether myself or Labib,
If a rival, why, for the pristine delight of your self-knowledge,
which walks, like the morning, in several voices?
Labib, the negation of every favoring voice!)
Yet ours is not a union of water and dust, nor ever was.
These elements have lived always outside Man,
nor was jar or pitcher always born of their union.
They can yield but one illusion,
let it be.

Jahanzad, you
he and I,
we, angles of an ancient triangle,
have always wandered, like the
turning of my potter's wheel,
but found no trace of ourselves.
If you wish, I'll break the triangle. But
The spell of the wheel on me is this old triangle:
The eyes of my wheel that stare at me,
turning.
On pitcher and jar your body, color, your tenderness
fell,

your beauty's alchemy
washing me in a flood of inner light.
Citizens of my inner world poured out into the streets,
As if hearing the cry of the morning *azan*.
All the pots in becoming, became "you."
This meeting's ecstasy has devoured me.
This is the crisis of cup, goblet, and pitcher—
cleaved from the essence of water and dust,
they achieve the triumph of new direction.

(I, a poor potter:
what do I know of this extreme
mystic intuition of
each cup, goblet, and pitcher?)

Jahanzad,
today I am waiting still, but why?
Just as I was for nine wretched years.
But now my waiting is not for the river of tears,
nor the wayward night
(I've talked so much of that night of sin
this too is now a sin)—
neither for the pool of the inn at Aleppo,
nor for Death, nor my broken self.
Yet in timeless waiting I am bound,
as moments arrive and pause in timeless time,
so this burden of time has fallen from my head.
All the dead, all past faces,
the sluggish caravans of all incidents
have awakened inside me
the stirring of a world regained,
as heaven awakes in the unconsciousness of God.
I woke, lying on the sand of drowsiness,

on the sand lay those pots,
outside my being,
shattered forever
in the chasm between me and myself.
They became whole once more (like some voice of providence).
They became once more a timeless dance,
a vision of eternity.

IV

Jahanzad, how after a thousand years,
scraps of my jars, enamels and flowerpots
are found
in every alley of a buried city,
as if they were its memory.
(A young potter, by the name of Hassan, in a new city,
still making pots, still loving,
was strung by us in the threads of his past,
with and within us—as though he were us—he is merged,
for you and I were the drops of rain,
that all through the night, a night stretching a thousand years,
falling across a windowpane continually traced snake lines,
and here, before the morning of time,
we and this youthful potter
are strung once more in a dream.)

Jahanzad, how
this crowd, worshippers of the past,
has entered the corpses of these pots,
see!
These are the people whose eyes
never pierced jar or pitcher.

Today, once again, they turn this way and that
The lifeless creations of color and oil.
Will they ever find, beneath these, the sparks of grief
that devoured history?
Will they ever hear the storms, the tempests
that devoured every scream?
What do they know of the rainbow that brought my colors—
mine and this young potter's?

What do they know of that butterfly's wings,
the qualities of that beauty, with which
I shaped the faces of these pots?
See these people, each his own prisoner.
The age, Jahanzad, is an enchanted tower
and these people are imprisoned in it.
The young potter laughs!
These naive savages, their garments torn
by their own stature, reaching for
some glory beyond reach,
what do they know of the demon, inevitable, in my heart's cave,
who forewarned me (and this young potter),
"Hassan the potter, awake!
The pains of prophethood have their day of reckoning,
which approaches your parched cups and pitchers!"
This is the call behind which, Hassan,
the young potter,
moves from age to age,
autumn to autumn,
unceasing.

Jahanzad, I, Hassan the potter, have
suffered this pain of prophethood in wilderness
after wilderness.

Will these people, a thousand years hence
reassembling the pieces, ever know
how the color and oil of my dust and earth
merged with your delicate limbs
to become eternity's voice?
Through my pores, every pore,
I would absorb
your expansive embraces,
I would make offerings
in the temple of the eyes of those to come.
Should they trace the art and culture of these fragments, so be it,
how shall they ever bring back Hassan the potter?
Or count the drops of his sweat,
or find even the shadow of this art's splendor?
Which has grown from age to age,
autumn to autumn,
which, in the new self of each potter,
ever grows?
The shadow of that art through which
none is anything but love,
none is anything but a potter?
We are full of knowledge, and know nothing.
We are, like God, wholly the gods of our art.
(Hopes are shallow and deep)
Faces swim in the eyes of senselessness,
faces never seen.
Where could their trace be found?
Who has ever honored the tradition of grief?

The corpses of these pots,
etceteras of some mortal story,
are our *azan*, the sign of our inquiry.
In the silence of their hour of death they speak:

"We are the eyes which open inwardly,
which gaze at you, seeking out every pain,
knowing the secret of each beauty.
We are the longing of that night's empty room,
where one face, like a tree branch,
leaning over another,
had left in each human heart
a rose petal.
We are that night's stolen kiss."

Translated from Urdu by M.A.R. Habib

FAIZ AHMAD FAIZ

A Prison Evening

From the winding maze of evening stars,
step by step descends the night.
The breeze passes close by, thus,
as if someone murmurs a word of love.
The exiled trees of the prison yard,
heads bent, are engrossed in drawing
patterns and sketches on the sky's skirt.
On the roof's shoulder gleams
the fair hand of moonlight's affection.
The glitter of stars has dissolved in dust,
the sky's blue melted in a splendor of light.
In green corners, shadows of blue
bloom, as in the heart
the pain of separation surges.
Constantly, thought reassures the heart:
so sweet is life at this moment.
Those who stir tyranny's poison
will succeed neither today nor tomorrow.
So what if they have already extinguished
the candles in the bridal chamber of love?
Show us if they can put out the moon!

Translated from Urdu by Waqas Khwaja

At the Sinai Valley

Once again lightning flashes across the Sinai Valley,
once again a flame blazes on reality's face—
the invitation to behold that reality, a message of death.
O far-seeing eye
Now is the time to witness, even if the spirit is flagging.
Now the executioner has become also the physician of grief's distress,
the garden of Iram looks like desolation's wasteland.
Has passion's pride
the courage to travel the road of annihilation or not?
Again lightning flashes across the Sinai Valley.
O far-seeing eye
wipe clean your heart once more. Perhaps on its tablet
some new compact between I and Thou may be inscribed.
Today, oppression is the custom of the great and noble of this earth,
support of oppression, a convenience of religion's magistrate.
To reverse centuries of abject allegiance,
today, a decree of defiance must descend.

Translated from Urdu by Waqas Khwaja

Don't Ask Me, Dear, for That First Love Again

Don't ask me, dear, for that first love again—
I once believed life drew its light from you.
In the torment of your love, what cared I for time and fortune?
Your face affirmed the advent of spring,
the world had nothing to match your eyes:
if you were mine, destiny itself would bend before me.

It wasn't thus, I had only wished it so.
There are other cares in the world than love,
comforts other than the meeting of lovers.

The dark sorcery of unfolding centuries,
woven in satin, in brocades and silk,
bodies on sale everywhere in lanes and streets,
besmeared in dust and bathed in blood.
The eye is drawn to them too, ah, well!
You no doubt are lovely still, ah, well!

There are other cares in the world than love,
comforts other than the meeting of lovers.
Don't ask me, dear, for that first love again.

Translated from Urdu by Waqas Khwaja

Go Forth into the Streets Today in Your Fetters

A damp eye, a distraught life, is not
    enough,
the imputation of a secret passion, is
    not enough.
Go forth into the streets today in
    your fetters.

Your hands alight
entranced and dancing, go!
Dust in your head
bloodstains on your shirtfront, go!
The whole city of love
awaits you, go!

The city's chief
the ordinary masses
the arrow of blame
the stone of abuse
the unhappy morning
the failed day—
who else is their familiar
but us?
Who in the beloved's city
is clean anymore?
Who remains worthy
of the executioner's hand?

Pick up the goods of your heart
brokenhearted, let's go!
Ourselves, then, we may present
for execution, friends, let's go!

Translated from Urdu by Waqas Khwaja

My Heart, Fellow Traveler

My heart, fellow traveler,
it is again commanded
that you and I be banished
to call in lanes and byways
and turn to unknown places,
to find some sign or portent
of some loved one's message bearer
and ask of every stranger
news of our home and homeland—
in streets of unknown people
to tend the day to darkness,
a word exchanged with this,
sometimes that other person.
What shall I tell you of it?
The pain of night is fearful.
This too would be enough if we
could keep a count of sorrow.
What would we care for dying
were there no death tomorrow?

Translated from Urdu by Waqas Khwaja

We, Who Were Killed in the Dark Pathways

For Julius and Ethel Rosenberg

Longing for the flowers of your lips, we
offered ourselves to a dry gallows tree.
Yearning for the torches of your hands, we
were killed in the dimly lit pathways.

On crosses beyond our reach
the color of your lips leapt and flamed
the rapture of your locks continued to rain
the silver of your hands gleamed.

When tyranny's night dissolved in your paths
we slogged on, as far as our feet would go
a love song on our lips, a candle of grief in the heart.
Our grief was witness to your loveliness.
See, we have remained true to our witness,
we, who were killed in the dark pathways.

If we were fated to remain unfulfilled
our love was but of our own devising.
Who complains, then, if the paths of aspiration
all led to parting in the fields of execution?

Picking up our banners from these killing fields
other caravans of lovers will go forth
from whose journey of longing our steps
have shortened the passage of pain.

For whom, relinquishing our lives, we have made
sovereign the credit of your loveliness in the world—
we, who were killed in the dark pathways.

Translated from Urdu by Waqas Khwaja

USTAD DAMAN

He Knows Not What He Must Express

He knows not what he must express,
What all he utters when he speaks—

Here even a bald pye-dog believes
He is a moon no shadow cleaves.

Peerzada swoons with joy indeed,
When Bhutto calls him his Ganymede.

Mulla Whiskey then fills up his cup,
Though the drink is causing his head to flop.

He begins to clap quite like a clown,
When the crowd is about to shout him down.

And makes to walk as he prates his bit,
Stands up again when about to sit.

Translated from Punjabi by Waqas Khwaja

My Country Has Two Allahs

My country has two Allahs,
La ila and Martial Law!
One lives high above the skies,
The other on terra firma lies;
One is simply called Allah,
The other is named General Zia.
Three cheers for General Zia!
Bravo! Bravo! General Zia!

What fun for our lovely land,
Wherever we go armed forces stand.
It happened only yesterday,
And will again another day,
A hundred thousand quit the field,
To give up half their country's land.
Three cheers for General Zia!
Bravo! Bravo! General Zia!

Translated from Punjabi by Waqas Khwaja

Partition

We may not say it but know it well,
You lost your way. We too.

Partition has destroyed us friends.
You too, and us.

The wakeful have quite plundered us.
You slept the while, and we.

Into the jaws of death alive
You were flung. We too.

Life still may stir in us again:
You are stunned yet, and we.

The redness of the eyes betrays
You too have wept, and we.

Translated from Punjabi by Waqas Khwaja

Brother, Are You from Kunjah?

Brother, you're from Kunjah, aren't you?
Your name is Sharif?
I was just thinking, "He looks like him!"
What a blessed day this is—
God has united me with my brother.
Son, this is your uncle, your mother's brother.
You may not have recognized me,
but when we were young we used to play together.
My name is Niyamatay—
I'm Mehr Nur Din's granddaughter, his daughter's daughter.
Kinship depends on keeping in touch,
just as a well is no well without water running below.
Time was, we used to visit there, occasionally, for days on end,
now I pine to even see those places—
and, do you know, *mammi* got really upset with us over me?
You tell me, brother, what was my fault in all this?
Who was dearer to me than my maternal relations?
But daughters don't talk back to their parents,
they don't undo the locks of their modesty.
And parents, too—who is more precious to them than their
　　own children?
They can never think of doing any harm to them.
One may, however, slip into straitened circumstances.
When my father's failing eyes defeated his will,
storms of hardships swept upon us.
Even my mother's side started avoiding us.
Whenever they saw us,

instead of blooming with happiness, their faces pinched and hardened.
We were still unbaked vessels, and the fire was dying out—
everyone, everything, abandoned us.
His father clutched my father's arm
and, dying, my father gave him his word.
True, there is no compatibility of age between us,
but brother, you are wise, you understand:
the daughter who doesn't recognize her debt to her parents
is not fit to be considered human.
I just folded this thought in my heart and accepted the situation,
cultured the discarded milk the first wife had thrown up.
God approved of my patience
and blessed me with this son, lovely as the moon.
There it is, then, this is where I get off.
Why don't you too join me today—
stay the night in the home of a long-forgotten sister?
Oh well! Those who live are likely to meet again.
Please give my deep regards to everyone.

Translated from Punjabi by Muhammad Shahid and Waqas Khwaja

Today, I am wicked; today, I am a liar. My words are odd.
Virtue is retailed in your store; truth lies by your side.
If in such times too I were to sing songs of dancing eyes
and blow the conch of Balnath's disciple wherever I go—
pretending to be the fictional Ranjha, break into the very home
where I visit on trust, spirit away its women
and, with illicit pleasure, praise in delicious detail,
from head to toe, each part and feature of their bodies—
then you will consider me worthy indeed and sing my praises
and fawn over each and every couplet of mine?

If I say that you and I are born of the same Adam,
why then should one suffer in labor and the other rest in ease?
If I say that no one should be homeless in the world
or that no one forced to drudge and grind in old age,
if I say that we should all share whatever coarse food and salt we have,
that we should be as arms to each other to ease our burdens,
if I say that we should put away all matters of conflict and quarrel,
resolve everything through discussion and not render ourselves mad
    and breathless,
then I am the wicked one, the liar, my words strange—
virtue retails at your store, truth lies by your side.

Translated from Punjabi by Muhammad Shahid and Waqas Khwaja

Traveler

Your body, a mulberry limb in bloom, your arms like slender branches,
your lips are flowers of caper, your youth, the grove's shade.
This shade lasts not forever, only His name remains,
and Providence, my fair, has brought us to this town.
We will quickly spend the afternoon, we are not staying long:
we Yogis have no village or home, no place to sit and stay.
Who can settle down forever? This world is but an inn.
Like your youth, my fair, we are all traveling.

Translated from Punjabi by Muhammad Shahid and Waqas Khwaja

Tree of the Barren Waste

I am a leafy tree of the barren waste,
my shade is cool,
my fruit sweet.
Wayfarer passing by,
tired and weary,
come, rest a while,
eat of my fruit,
sit in my shade.
I am a leafy tree of the barren waste,
my shade is cool.

What matter if the road lies all ahead?
What matter if the day is in decline?
Granted, life's a baffling ordeal,
but burning thus beneath the sun,
swallowing dust,
makes little sense.
Those moments alone are pleasant
spent resting in the shade.

This shade, too, is brief,
brief like youth itself,
then leaves will fall—
come, now, and sit beneath them.
I am a leafy tree of the barren waste,
my shade is cool.

Translated from Punjabi by Muhammad Shahid and Waqas Khwaja

MEERAJI

Call of the Sea

Sounds whisper: "Come now, come! Years of calling and calling
have fatigued my soul."
For a moment, for an age, I have heard those voices,
which never tire of calling.
And now comes this curious voice:
"My sweet child, how I love you, see. But should you do this,
none would be harder on you than I." "Lord! Lord!"

They always come, these voices, in every shape,
in sobs, smiles, or frowns.
Through them this brief life meets eternity.
But this strange voice, full of fatigue,
threatens always to drown all others.

Now the eyes know no flicker, the face wears neither smile nor frown,
only the ears go on listening.
Here is a rose garden, where winds ripple, buds open, blossoms yield
fragrance,
flowers bloom, fade and fall, spreading a velvet floor
on which my longings move softly, like mythical fairies, mirrored in
the garden—
a mirror in which each face appeared, settled, and dissolved forever.
The mountain is silent and still,
though some fountain, rising, might ask what lies beyond these rocky
peaks.
But sufficient for me is the mountain's foot—at the foot, in the valley
a stream carries a boat—another mirror

in which each face clearly surfaced and dissolved forever.
Here is a desert—vast, parched, leafless,
here whirlwinds house fierce spirits.
But I am far away, my eyes focused on a grove of trees.

Now there is no desert, no mountain, no rose garden,
in the eyes no life, on the face no smile or frown,
merely a strange voice droning that it is exhausted calling.
Voices always calling.
So the voice is a mirror—it is only I who am weary.
No desert, no mountain, no rose garden:
the sea alone calls me.
All comes from the sea, all will return.

Translated from Urdu by M.A.R. Habib

Strange Waves of Pleasure

I want the world's eyes to watch me, as if
watching a tree's tender branch,
(a tree's tender, yielding branch),
its leafy burden heaped, like cast-off clothes, on the floor
beside the bed.
I wish the gusts of wind would embrace me over and over—
peevish, teasing, saying something laughingly,
hesitant, heavy with shyness, steadying themselves in amorous,
    honeyed, whispers.
I want to go on, walking, running,
just as the wind, rustling, caressing the stream's surface,
continues to blow unceasingly.
If a bird should sing in charming notes,
let the warm waves of sound ring against my body and return,
    without pause.
Warm rays, gentle breezes,
sweet, enthralling words—
new things, ever new colors, that arise,
arise and dissolve in the surrounding air.
Let nothing cease within the circle of my rapture.
The circle shrinks,
the open field of wheat spreads out,
far out, the sky's strange pavilion, transforming itself into an exotic
    bed,
tempts with seductive gestures.
The sound of lapping waves melts into birdsong, and slipping away
vanishes now from the eyes.

I am sitting,
my scarf slipped from my head.
I don't care if anyone sees my hair!
The circle of pleasures contracts.
Let nothing new enter the circle of my rapture.

Translated from Urdu by M.A.R. Habib

Tall Building

Eyes painted in thousands on your face,
you are a standing monument
that guards the civilized,
your body moonlight,
a storm that wells up,
a whirlwind in man's mind.

In the crashing waves
rage songs of tyranny,
a keening dirge
that lingers in the shadow of mourning,
words that speak without dreaming.
Is a soul lamenting restlessly in your heart?

The waves of your song weaken,
their ripples fade away. And I begin to see
dregs clouding bitter wine in a cracked cup.
Intoxication clouds my eyes.
Why does the night's spilling darkness scare me so?
Your flickering eyes don't:
I've lived in greater darkness,
And in this darkness of the soul, shone stars of sorrow;
And sometimes, every star, forgetfully, flared in flames of comfort
that leap, arms open, from your windows like the notes of your song,
as if drawn into the shawl of space.
I recall now the tears I spilled in desolation,
those tears, those flames of comfort.

But it was just a dream, and the leaping of flames was like a dream.
The wings of my imagination, like a bird's broken wings,
fluttered uselessly.
The tension of my limbs would not let me breathe;
stirring just once, desire suggested to me the possibility of release.
But, alas, when grief was about to become its own medicine,
my shackles were lifted
to calm my nerves—
forgetting my tears, I recovered my lost spirit
and climbed that height
on which you stand blinking your innumerable eyes.

I had been told strange tales about you.
I had heard that your large body houses a bed
on which a delectable woman rests
her loneliness seeping into her mind like bland fatigue.
But she's restless as she waits
for the curtain to move
and her dress to slide away like a cloud.
When an unknown man appears at the door
she doesn't care
whether his manners please her or not
because she wants only one thing from him—
that he erects, from the sea of nerves,
a curious figure,
whose appearance is loathsome
and who, in a moment, becomes your adversary,
the brain seized by a storm,
and that woman, uninhibited, untainted, undesigning,
comes to resemble a falling wall.
Forgetting the song of her fatigue,
she knocks down
the soulless spectator of night like a palace of sand

with a brief movement of her eye;
the curious figure created by the sea of nerves,
collapses like a falling wall.

These tales, in the form of fleeting fragrances,
used to dance in my mind
whenever they wished.

Now in those innumerable eyes of yours
I see but one, shining.
Does the flame of comfort burn in that eye?

I want to close that eye with my hand, now.

Translated from Urdu by Geeta Patel

MAJEED AMJAD

An Individual

What can I accomplish in this vast order by my one act of goodness?
I can't do more than that—
my whole world on a table:
paper, pen, and broken, shattered poems.
I have arranged them all neatly.
My heart is full of so many good things.
When I think of them, these very breaths seem priceless.
What strange things are these in which I find consolation!
Finding me true to the consolation,
all falsehoods come to attest my cause.
If only I were true,
those things arranged neatly in my world
would be replaced by disordered pieces,
pieces of my body beneath the rocking saw of black lies.
My one good deed could confront this vast order,
if I indeed were true.

Translated from Urdu by Mehr Afshan Farooqi

Little Children

Little children, I remember when I was your age,
how good they were who were older than we,
honest and gracious.
Little children, when you are as old as I am
those who were older than you
will have long since gone to sleep beneath the earth.
I wonder what you will think of us then?
Perhaps those days will be difficult, but you will at least remember
what a people they were who sank in their own blood
but let no harm come to this land
where today the gardens of your aspirations bloom.

Translated from Urdu by Mehr Afshan Farooqi

On the Radio, a Prisoner Speaks . . .

On the radio, a prisoner speaks to me: "I am safe!
Listen . . . I'm alive!"
Brother . . . so, who is he addressing? When are *we* alive?
Having traded your sacred life for this glittery existence,
we died a long while ago.

We are in this graveyard—
we don't even look up from our graves.
What do we know of the lamps of lament
your heartbreaking cries have lit?
In their light the world is now trying to make out our names
    on these tombstones.

Translated from Urdu by Mehr Afshan Farooqi

A Cry

Black-beaked, with blue and yellow plumage,
the twittering *lali* cried, "Cheep, cheep!" "Tweet, tweet!"
Settling down, then suddenly taking off,
flying, wheeling in the air,
she alighted on a power line,
swaying on the swing of death.

A scream arose from my heart. I cried out,
loud as a kettledrum.
At my call the *lali* spread her wings and flew from the threshold of death,
that bird with the blue and yellow wings.

And then there's you,
sitting in burning fire and lost in dreams of flowers.
Every scream from my heart calls out to you in vain.

Translated from Urdu by Mehr Afshan Farooqi

Solicitation

Filled with noise of brisk footsteps
a pathway with lawns and meadows on either side
a paradise of colors all around.

Hundreds of flowerbeds toward which
no passerby casts a glance.
A branch laden with crimson flowers

leans out, spreads itself across the path
rubs her forehead on the gravel
touches the feet of passersby:

"I don't come by every day.
My time to go is almost here.
I beg you, look my way."

Translated from Urdu by Mehr Afshan Farooqi

Sons of Stony Mountains

Sons of those regions of my land where, for centuries, treeless rocks
  have stood alone,
where only harsh seasons and a lifelong flood of pain exist—

Sons of stony mountains,
glowing jasmine petals, fragments of jagged rock,
gentle, soft, milky white bodies, and hard, rough, darkened hearts.
Seared by sun and wind,
fallen from the cliffs, they search for their homeland in the dust
  beneath their feet.

Homeland—a pile of unwashed dishes—
that sweating labor searches from place to place.

Homeland—traveling darkness that,
pausing in towns by streams that tumble from high mountains,
has become smoke rising from some tin roof.

The stream, sprinkled gold dust, and the smoke, sprinkled gold dust.
But in the priceless current of sweat and water,
if those who would kill conscience were to appraise
the surge of pain that is the measure of life,
the black rocks of hearts would melt.

Translated from Urdu by Mehr Afshan Farooqi

Spring

Every time, in the same way, the world
molds flower buds of yellow mustard from a lump of gold,
and the breeze holds them in its undulations.

Every time, in the same way, branches
laden with bourgeoning shoots,
leaning against spikes of fences along the way . . . what do they think?
   Who knows.

Every time, in the same way, raindrops
filtering through clouds brimming with color
come to rattle against the copper sheet that spreads into the distance.

Every year, a season, just like this,
every time, this scent of absence,
every morning, these harsh tears. When will the times of mourning come?

Translated from Urdu by Mehr Afshan Farooqi

GUL KHAN NASEER

I Am a Rebel

I am fire, lightning, sword
I am cannon, bomb, vengeance
challenge, proclamation, embodiment of God's will
I fight the tyrant
I am a rebel, I am a rebel

Fettered, they, but I am free
Not the ruled, I am the ruler
not deceitful, I bring relief
not a thief
I am a rebel, I am a rebel

Gold and silver are not my gods
I don't barter away my country
nor do I bark for a piece of bread
I toil and labor
I am a rebel, I am a rebel

Arrows and guns are but toys to me
I drive thieves into the hereafter
decree servility a crime and sin
seize freehold grants
I am a rebel, I am a rebel

I fight for rights
I color my land with my blood
I squeeze my enemy

I tell the truth
I am a rebel, I am a rebel

I keep a close eye on predators
I uproot injustice and cruelty
I am my motherland
free from bondage
I am a rebel, I am a rebel

Workers must remain united
The wealth of life I am willing to sacrifice
I am a rebel, I am a rebel

Translated from Balochi by Azmat Ansari and Waqas Khwaja

Towering Ramparts

Towering ramparts of stone and brick,
with strong doors and chains of steel—
jails and prisons have been created, but nothing
can confine high ideals.

Even if tyrants and oppressors, no matter where,
are able to construct such forts
and torture
inmates in fetters and stocks
and fill up the prison cells,
the light of high ideals
will fall beyond prison walls
and the hearts of freedom-loving youth
be illuminated by those who have embraced the struggle.

The ministers appointed by tyrants
intoxicated by their addiction to silver and gold,
proud of their cannons and guns,
indulge in murder and slaughter—
but against people mad with rage
their power and money are impotent.
Nor does the slippery talk of these brokers
hold up against the conflagration
that rises from the inflamed breast
and, through the guidance of the wise,
mingles with the surging blood
descending like lightning on prison houses.

The fury and vehemence of the seething population,
like a fire that sweeps through a forest,
like an ocean tempest
or raging torrents of monsoon rains,
will burn to ash and wash away
jails, prisons, and forts,
masters and their palaces—
blow them away like dust and ash,
to clear the space for a new world.

Towering ramparts of stone and brick,
with strong doors and chains of steel—
jails and prisons have been created, but nothing
can confine high ideals.

Translated from Balochi by Azmat Ansari and Waqas Khwaja

Will Not Be Silent

O my mortal enemy! Alive, I will not be silent
As long as a tongue moves in my mouth, I will not be silent

You can kill, you can burn and tyrannize
Yet even on the gallows I will speak the truth: I will not be silent

I am not a moth that goes up suddenly in flame
I am a candle that burns until morning: I will not be silent

As long as the fire in my breast does not consume
desert and mountain, I will not be silent

As long as my brave young fighters do not overturn
the world of greed and profit, I will not be silent

As long as peasants, with their own peaceful labor
are unable to fill their bellies, I will not be silent

As long as cowherds and camel drivers
are hungry and discontent, I will not be silent

As long as I do not tear up from its roots the world
of my masters, I will not be silent

How long can the tortures of prison silence me?
Even in a rain of arrows I will not be silent

Consumed by fire, body exhausted, heart broken in two
Even so, if there is one breath of life, I will not be silent

I have given a rake's word to Naseer
I shall have freedom or death—I will not be silent

Translated from Balochi by Azmat Ansari and Waqas Khwaja

GHANI KHAN

Devadasi

Doves coo and robins sing,
the gentle wind blows playfully in waves.
Morning comes with laughter and light
as flower buds exclaim in joy, "What a delight is the breeze!"
Time reaches another stopping place, another night recedes—
one spent it with a lover, another sobs, alone.
All night I sat in a world of many hues,
mixing color and sensation to paint and draw.
Enchanted by some pretty face, I drank the sorrows of the heart;
her looks withered, she lost all color.
Should I paint Layla, or Shirin, or Mansur?
In every eye, I am there—my pain, my dreams.
I take two colors, black and red, and paint Chengiz or Timur:
the fury in their eyes leaps from the fire of my own.
Into this burning madness, a sorrowful goddess arrives—
not Layla, Shahai, Hira, or Shirin.
Her beauty, a poet's dream!
Her heavy eyes, stricken by grief, drunk with longing,
each look, each gesture, caught in the glow of youthful desire,
her presence luminous, the color of new love.
"Look at me, painter," she said, "at what I am!
A wretched *devadasi*, that most humble of creatures."
"You are the very daughter of beauty," I replied, "a brilliant princess!
For your burning eyes, one would renounce a thousand thrones.
Mistress of sorrows, you are a goddess born of blossoming flowers.
In the bloom of spring and youth, why these autumnal colors?
Your lips are not lips, but a libation of desire,

secret vintner, a tempest lies in each drop of your wine.

What dark, forbidding mountains exist in this lovely world!

You are a slender rose branch, and autumn is still far.

Let be your twenty masks, but discard the one of grief—

let laughter enter your garden and brighten the world.

You are not a stone image! You are the slave of a stone image: your eyes
     glitter.

You are wine and *saqi* both—intoxicate your lover!

What is beauty without one to admire it? What is love without a lover?

The world that cannot see your splendor is without eyes.

Devotion, love, and desire light every movement, every gesture of yours.

But a grim design has shadowed your life's candescent passion.

Come and sit beside me, I am kin to your desire!

You are a desert flower—I, too, am one,

I, too, aggrieved, afflicted, obliged by life to weep.

Blood and love, they both cry, in yearning for a lover."

Looking at me, she smiled, but her eyes brimmed with tears.

Holding tight her black shawl, quietly she walked away.

Her hope, her longing, twinkled like a guiding star

wandering the desert in search of roses.

In the dancer's step, in the grace of the branching rose,

I lost the world of passion and beauty when I recovered my sense.

She left in my heart a new pain and a bright heat,

a golden particle of radiance from the light infusing the world.

Translated from Pashto by Sher Zaman Taizi and Waqas Khwaja

O Ghani! O You Ass, Ghani!

O Ghani! O you ass, Ghani!
Ghani of Hashtnagar!
Humble Ghani, grand Ghani,
Both the same, Ghani—
Ghani of plains and hills,
of land and sea, Ghani!
Are you aware, Ghani,
is the heart in charge, or is it the head, Ghani?
You will never bow to anyone
your proud head, Ghani!
What is this street of goldsmiths, Andhar Shahr,
where no one recognizes gold, Ghani?
Senseless even when sane,
your drunken head, Ghani!
When sober, flushed—
not worth calling a head, Ghani!
When and why, Ghani?
Come tell me soon, Ghani.
A star shining far away
catches my eye, Ghani.
Friend, let us go there—
you have grown wings, Ghani!
O Khan of Khans, Ghani!
O Ghani! O you ass, Ghani!
Life, Ghani, distraction, Ghani,
eyes and eyesight, Ghani!
Keep love, beloved, and beauty—

let all else pass, Ghani.
Stay away from lakes and whirlpools
lest you tumble in and perish, Ghani.
The hunt lasts a lifetime,
in the end the prey will fall, Ghani!
The love of humanity,
like heavenly Kausar from barren sands, Ghani!
Nowhere further to go—
this is the mountain peak, Ghani.
Sit down, calm yourself,
forget your cares, O my heart, Ghani!
This is the desert of love,
don't leave it, Ghani.
Friend, where were you deceived, alas?
O Ghani! O you ass, Ghani!
You gave the call for morning prayer—
it is afternoon, Ghani!
O Ghani! O you ass, Ghani!
Ghani of Hashtnagar! O Ghani!

Translated from Pashto by Pervez Sheikh and Waqas Khwaja

Question or Answer

Speak, mullah, speak!
Is life a question or answer?
Is it a consummation of love or a mad obsession?
Rest or agitation?
Is life an imam or a lover?
The pulpit or the throne room?
Or, in a wayward world,
the mirage of a beautiful dream?
A moment to snatch light
from the darkness of the universe?
Is life question or answer?
Speak, mullah, speak!
Life is pharaoh and presumption—
or is it madness and ecstasy?
Is it Nimrod's throne of gold,
or the lurid death of Mansur?
Lovely, full of smiles,
or Yazid, swelling with pride?
Is it spring, or the rose,
half hidden from the eye?
Is life question or answer?
Speak, mullah, speak!
An intoxicating cup of wine,
or a beggar's broken bowl?
The fuddled face of Khayyam,
or the shrewd countenance of the fool Bahlol?
A rose garden splashed with color,

or a hedge of fiery thorns?
Is it escape or flight?
Flight from oneself?
Is life question or answer?
Speak, mullah, speak!
Life is beauty that spreads—
or is it beauty that vanishes?
Music that laments its own demise,
or a flaming fire?
Is there a resting place on the way,
or merely breath in pursuit of another breath?
Or is it buckets on a water wheel,
some empty, some full?
Or light expanding endlessly,
unaware of its glory?
Is life question or answer?
Speak, mullah, speak!

Translated from Pashto by Sher Zaman Taizi and Pervez Sheikh

Search

a summer noon
like winter night
silence
and tranquility
the soft cooing of doves
nothing stirs, nothing moves
time pauses
with its foot in the stirrup
the world attends its beating heart
auditing accounts of life and death
a smile haunts the atmosphere
as of one hearing the *rabab* in a dream
and I, alone
sunk in
my grief
go about seeking
a lost
helpless
traveler—
lying on the ground
I travel
the skies
I, too, listening to my heartbeat
seeking the root and cause of life
the argument for pain and death
why? and for what?
lost in rivers

in the wine cup
and in the wine
in the flame-red book
on the shelf in a mosque—
for death and life
I seek a connection
quietly, secretly
in silence
I . . .
in the notes of the sitar
I seek the theme
in the colors all around
in slate-gray pigeons
I seek the meaning of my existence
I am mad, mad indeed
seeking Plato in the tavern
when I turn my eyes to myself
only
death
negation and absence
I see
I am mad, mad indeed
seeking life in the eyes of death
a summer noon
like winter night
silence
and tranquility
somewhere, far away
a spark
of light
a star
or a fire out in the desert
says

to me
with its tiny rays
"if a mountain is high
a passage runs through it"
what
if life
is a lost
moment
of awareness?
one
eternal
beloved it has for company
O heart! do you deceive yourself or me?
how can I extricate myself from these tangles?
O heart! O deceiving heart!
you engage yourself in pleasing me
but if I ignore what you say
I am ruined
yes, truly
I will go mad
in the black waters of bewilderment
now I swim, now sink
I lose my way in the dark
here, in my own fire, burn
living, I decay and turn to dust
drown in my own blood
the summer noon
like winter night
silence, and tranquility
far away, somewhere
a spark of light
a star, or a fire out in the desert
says to me with its tiny rays

"if a mountain is high, a passage runs through it"
what if life is a lost moment of awareness?
an eternal beloved it has for company

Translated from Pashto by Sher Zaman Taizi and Pervez Sheikh

AHMAD NADEEM QASMI

A Prayer for the Homeland

God grant that on my pure land should alight
a harvest of flowers that fears no decline

the flower that blossoms here may bloom for centuries
and autumn has never to pass this way

the green that sprouts here may remain forever green
and such a green that it is without compare

heavy clouds may bring down such rains
that even stones become verdant and fruitful

God grant that my country's honored head may never bend
and its beauty have no dread of passing time

that each person arrive at the summit of art and culture
that no one be unhappy, no one live in distress

God grant that for not one of my compatriots
should life be an ordeal, affliction, or crime

God grant that on my pure land should alight
a harvest of flowers that fears no decline

Translated from Urdu by Omer Khwaja

Stone

Don't make statues with sand, my good artist!
Wait a moment, I will bring you stones.
I will pile them up before you, but
which color of stone would you like to use?

Red—that is called heart by a heartless world?
Or that blue of a petrified eye
streaked with centuries of amazement?

Will you need the soul's stone,
on which truth itself falls like a stone?
Then there is that stone called white civilization—
in its marble, black blood can be glimpsed.
There is also the stone of justice, but
it is secured only if the adze of gold is in hand.
All the standards of this age are stone,
all the opinions of this world are stone,
poetry, dance, painting, song—all are stone,
my imagination, your quick intellect, stone as well—
in this age the sign of every art is stone,
your hands are stone, my tongue is stone.
Don't make statues with sand, my good artist.

Translated from Urdu by Omer Khwaja

WAZIR AGHA

Terminus

There was nothing there
just a tiny square
steel cabin
that served as office, residence, and ticket booth,
all together.
Outside the cabin, straight ahead, in the line of vision,
was a red signal post,
and beneath that red signal
black rail tracks
striking into the breast of a hill
had apparently just come to a halt—
for thousands of years,
just there, at the foot of Chhanni Khachi,
lying inert.

There's a rumor,
just a rumor, that when
evening fell
a strong breeze blew
and classes were declared over for the day,
the schoolmaster's turban
came off the peg
and, turning into a black cobra,
sat curled upon the treasure,
and that treasure of wisdom, of knowledge and skill
stood up with the support of a stick
and cleared his throat like a silver vessel.

Then we—pale children,
coins of some future age,
tumbling, clattering—rolled out
into the lanes, into the four corners of our village.
Our pleasant houses
like a till
drew us to themselves.

But we were not the coins of the till.
In the vicissitudes of time, we had yet
to declare our own worth.
In our mysterious, cool gleaming, we
were yet to pass through the touch of many fingertips—
we were in circulation, moving!

So that when night fell
and a sharp wind blew
we entreated our Baba:
Show us, too, the Chhanni Khachi station some time!
They say that a hill there presides
over the tracks like an ascetic *jogan* over a smoking fire—
she stands by the entrance, mysterious, queer,
with her hair undone like a witch.
Take us with you, show us the witch—
show us Chhanni Khachi!
Us—promise us,
Baba, promise us!

And Baba, clasping us to his breast, would say:
What will you do there?
What is there to see?
There is just a red steel cabin
and beyond that cabin

where the railway tracks stop
a black wooden signboard
that reads
"Nothing beyond this point."
My dear children!
I don't know how long
I've been standing in front of this signboard.
Look at me carefully before you decide,
but decide for yourselves.

But we puffed up our faces and said:
No! We know nothing of this!
Show us Chhanni Khachi!

Us—promise us,
Baba! Promise us!

And then one day
holding on to our Baba's finger
we boarded the train from our village
and a wave of happiness
swept through the depths of our bodies.
Hearts beat fast,
became a part of the swift engine's *choo choo choo choo*—
we felt as if the engine
were our body,
the train, a shadow
that pursued us,
lurching, straightening, dragging itself along.

Then it happened
that the train's windows beckoned us
and showed us a scene strange and marvelous.

We saw that the whole earth
was covered with stalks of rice.
Flights of birds,
surveying the earth with hungry eyes, shook their wings.
Above the birds
were scattered the rags
of some soft, silky cloudlets.
A little beyond that
the sky's azure body
was visible to everyone
through rents in the torn cloak of clouds.
Instantly, in the thick garment of "we"
a slit emerged,
grew wider and became a window,
and then "I,"
stepping through the window, asked:
Do you have any idea
what else is there beyond the sky?
And I turned back

and gazed at birds, cloudlets, and earth,
at the engine spewing smoke
and the train tied to the hem of the engine's shirt,
at my Baba in the compartment,
at others who sat beside Baba,
gazed long at everyone.
And in that lucid moment
I,
transformed into a glittering dewdrop
trembling on the earth's eyelash,
began to perceive my separate existence—

began to perceive my separate existence—
then I became afraid.

Catching the smell of Chhanni Khachi, the black engine,
overcome with delight, had let out a shriek
and yet another shriek,
and his black locks
flying backwards

caressed the body and limbs of the dragging train.
Smoke had filled the belly of the train.
But then, suddenly, my Baba,
waking out of a stupor, said to me:
There, the journey's over!
Come along now—
the train is about to stop, get your things together.
Step down, look at it,
and quench your thirst!
But I was already up.
The moment the train stopped with a hiccup
I leaned outwards
and put my foot
into some blind, barren atmosphere.
Just thus, for a second I remained suspended in air
and then stepped to the ground,
landing at the last frontier of palpitating time.

On Chhanni Khachi's stretched
frozen eyebrow
like a petal of snow I came to rest.
I saw
there was emptiness all around me,
no clue to where my Baba had fallen behind,
no engine, no railcars,
smoke, fire, speed . . . nothing whatsoever.
Only the railway tracks remained

that lay like an expired moment on the ground.
But I was no expired moment.
Below the crest of my dry hair,
above my parched lips,
screened by quivering curtains
two windows were opening up.
From these windows, in vacant space, in the
    mist,
Chhanni Khachi's square steel cabin, the signal
and the hill below the signal that had
abruptly cut off the black railway tracks—all of it,

in rising spectral shapes I
was beginning to recognize.
But then, all at once, sight
returned to my eyes in a blaze
such that beyond the hill
through the rent in the thick mist
I saw a handsome, frothy river,
that like a rough, untamed horse
sped on in angry leaps,
on which no saddle
or black, heavy, steel bridge
slung its weight.

I don't know how long,
lost in that scene of bounding and leaping
tied to the string of my sight,
I would have remained besieged,
when over the river,
wet from some slick rock, a bird took off,
flew to the far side of the river.

And then
my amazed, sharp, shining
eyes saw
that there, on that riverbank too,
was a red signal
a square steel cabin
and railway tracks, on that side too,
lying like an expired moment on the ground,
spreading out their naked arms
toward the river,
inert, unfeeling.

Then, in that instant of awareness
another flashing light, descending from somewhere,
took me in its lap and said:
When there is no bridge
between "here" and "there,"
between rusted past and spanking clean
time yet to be,
the suspended moment of "now,"
this signal, the wall of this hill,
the steel room,
will forever endure at a single point.
In time's unending string
Chhanni Khachi is a knot.
If the knot unravels
nothing will remain.

But today I think
I, too, was a tiny little knot,
and in my self Chhanni Khachi was hiding.
If that day I had crossed the bridge of that moment,
I would not have been able to stop.

If the swift river, with its spray of foam,
had given me the way,
I would have advanced
through vacancies of space

and begged only for charity
from every echo and sound I heard.
I—between the shores of beginning and eternity,
nameless, directionless,
clinging to
the broken stirrups of a rough, untamed horse—
would have been wandering forever,
wandering forever.

Translated from Urdu by Waqas Khwaja

SHEIKH AYAZ

Dialogue

Wadera: I have milked my buffaloes,
        steam rises from the cooking pot.
        Is there lightning outside?
        Is it raining outside?

Hari: My intestines coil with hunger, the fire
        in my kitchen is out.
        Is there lightning outside?
        Is it raining outside?

Wadera: I have my father's heifers and bullocks of good breed
        that impregnate my cows.
        Is there lightning outside?
        Is it raining outside?

Hari: I have neither cows nor father's heifers
        and no worry about cows getting pregnant.
        Is there lightning outside?
        Is it raining outside?

Wadera: My *autaq* has a solid roof,
        and if there's lightning outside, let there be lightning,
        and if it rains outside, let it rain.

Hari: My hut has a blue roof and it clatters loudly.
        Lightning? Let lightning be all the more.
        Rain? Let the rain pour!

Translated from Sindhi by Asif Farrukhi and Shah Mohammed Pirzada

Farewell to the Earth

Now I ask leave—
farewell!
I put the bow
to rest—
farewell!

I will sing
my last song,
like a flickering flame
ready to go out.
Farewell!
Those caravans
that have already departed,
I am going further than they.
Farewell!
But where am I going?
I do not know.

In the distance
the evening beckons me.
I will go and
immerse myself in it—
farewell!

With so many pains,
so many sorrows,
still, life was worth loving,

and lovely
was the moonlight
on midnight trees.
Today, I step
into the sky,
toward the moon—
farewell!

Like rain clouds I go,
having poured myself on the *thar*.
But this instrument,
slung over my shoulder—
how long can I keep on playing it?
Farewell!

Farewell, my Sindh!
Farewell, my Hind!
All the world
was contained in you.
Farewell, my life,
farewell!

Translated from Sindhi by Asif Farrukhi and Shah Mohammed Pirzada

Horse Rider

O horse rider!
    Where do you go?

No tavern or inn for you to rest.
A winter evening—the cold air
pierces and stabs like a dagger.

O horse rider!
    Where do you go?

You never pull up the reins
at any watering hole,
though you see lamps lit bright along the way,
and the stars arrayed against the sky.

    Where do you go?

Your feet forever suspended, not touching the earth,
your head not reclining in anyone's lap—
pause your headlong journey while you can.

    Where do you go?

O horse rider!
O horse rider!

Translated from Sindhi by Asif Farrukhi and Shah Mohammed Pirzada

Write

"Have you ever fought a war? Have you seen
bodies falling in dust?"

"Yes."

"Then write about it."

"Have the lips of a bride ever played
like a flute on your lips?"

"Yes."

"Then write about it."

"Have you ever closed your eyes after getting drunk
and felt the river swing and sway,
and have you ever glided across it like a swan?"

"Yes."

"Then write about it."

"Has your goal ever moved within reach,
then just as suddenly drifted away,
silencing your heart like a drum?"

"Yes."

"Then write about it. Don't write only
of things you have heard. Don't write
only from reading what others have written."

Translated from Sindhi by Asif Farrukhi and Shah Mohammed Pirzada

Gently Blows the Breeze

Trees sway, eyes cannot sleep,
gently blows the breeze.
My longing for a swindler has deceived me,
gently blows the breeze.

They tire not in waiting,
eyes never weary,
no longer can they bear his absence.
Desire for him, and fear of the world!
Gently blows the breeze.
My longing for a swindler has deceived me,
gently blows the breeze.

Laughing, I can hide from others,
dissembling, lying,
but where can I flee from my heart?
The light of love burns clear and bright,
gently blows the breeze.
My longing for a swindler has deceived me,
gently blows the breeze.

I go at dawn to fetch water.
My heart flutters—
What if seizing my arm he calls me
and the smoldering heap suddenly flares up?
Gently blows the breeze.
My longing for a swindler has deceived me,

gently blows the breeze.
Trees sway, eyes cannot sleep,
gently blows the breeze.

Translated from Punjabi by Amritjit Singh and Waqas Khwaja

Spinning Party

Why should I spin, why weave, mother of sorrows?
Today the courtyard lies forsaken,
for a band of traveling peddlers
has stolen the clink of bangles—
a bonfire of sighs, mother,
for the laughter of virgins today.
Which way should I go—
forward, backward, left or right?
On every side Kaidos or Kheras
Who have harried a hundred thousand Heers,
A hundred thousand Ranjhas burned alive.
With whom can I share my woes,
mother of tears?
I spin and weep continually,
pulling bobbin after spooled bobbin.
I ache for my father's home
and twice as much I miss my brothers,
but to whom shall I reveal my heart's anguish?
No one shares my pain.
Separated from my brothers,
I sigh endlessly—my father's house
is but a dream today,
the spinning sisterhood now a party of one.
Even the wheel's hum
startles and alarms me.
With balls of cotton thread, dear mother,
I wipe my weeping eyes,
but my tears refuse to dry,

mother of hope.
No henna traced on my palms,
no good luck threads or bracelets,
no friends sang my wedding songs,
no sisters-in-law applied the kohl,
no groom arrived wearing a wedding headdress
nor brothers blessed my departing *doli*—
whomever could seize another's arm
dragged her away.
Snakes hiss on all sides,
a hundred thousand tears cry out,
but no one hears their voice.
Those who set fire with their own hands,
they who dwell in palaces and mansions,
all God's creation is in their hands.
In state assemblies and courts,
they sit adjusting their turbans,
sit tall and upright.
What do they know of our grief?
We are but serfs, mere hired hands—
they, lords of the land,
mother of desires.
If, breaking into their mansions,
traveling peddlers were to steal
the clink of bangles,
then would I see, dear mother,
how these lords of the land,
they who dwell in mansions and palaces,
sit in state assemblies and courts
adjusting their turbans,
sit tall and upright!

Translated from Punjabi by Amritjit Singh and Waqas Khwaja

Portents of Good Tidings

I

I harbor a beautiful dream but am miserable
The heart dreads all auspicious signs

Flower bud, open your eye, gradually
Unfold little by little, slowly

Look! Lift your eyelashes and see
hearts split, wounds unhealed

Eyes sunk in an abyss of lamentation
Life ashamed of life itself

Our shattered dreams in heaps
bodies worn out, the spirit undone

Life, a desert of quicksand
Profitless grief, a consumptive chest

All desires unsatisfied
All regrets deadly

The eye's pageants, a fleeting moment
The darkness of pain, unremitting

Flower bud of yearning, unfold slowly
The heart frets at every auspicious sign

II

When bare branches had turned black
not a trace of sap left in their veins
the claws of predatory winds
that scratch and tear at the feathers of trees
retreated somewhere within soft paws

On the frozen lake
here and there on a sheet of ice
crystal circles of blue water
like glittering eyes
began to stir
and from the hand of melting ice
on all four sides the shore's garment began to slip
Slowly, the lake became a mirror

On the stems of dry branches
knots like half-closed eyes broke open
to reveal
tiny flames of sprouting nubs
candles of soft unfolding buds
the harbingers of spring
Then suddenly
somewhere a fierce squall produced a gale
windstorms worked their havoc and destruction
branches everywhere shook and fell

Many times we have seen
before the arrival of springtime
seasons of spring obliterated
Now, again, spring approaches
and, again, I am afraid of the portents
Flower bud, open your eye, gradually
Unfold little by little, slowly

Translated from Urdu by Omer Khwaja

Autumn's days are gone
Now, I ruminate
They were strange days, strange times, when eyes
peeked through the curtains of the imagination into
every nook and corner of the past
Days of autumn, as if someone in mature age
were content with the achievements of youth
Autumn, as if someone, in the sunlight of late afternoon,
    were enjoying a light sleep
as if drowsiness were brushing the eyelashes with its
    silky fingers
and, in this welcome tranquility, waves of a light breeze
    as if patting gently to sleep
The days of autumn were strange days
The petals of blooming flowers, long since fallen, had
    become one with dust and chaff
But those flowers were now gleaming fruit
that, heavy with nectar, glowed on bough and limb
This was fruit that the wind's currents could never
    trouble
Eyes that once awaited spring
had now arrived at a fixed point
The days of autumn, as if some artist had perfected
    his art
On the wind's tides even dry leaves had lost themselves
    in a song—

Here go the dry leaves, here they go
accompanying the wind, vagrants, nomads
away from these now desolate gardens
away from the canopy of trees
in whose arms they once grew and flourished
Here go the dry leaves, here they go
the caravan rolls, away from its past
remembering no more the moonlit night of bliss
nor anything from crowded gatherings
those days remain no more, gone are those tumults
    and passions
Here go the dry leaves, here they go
going where nothing will be
no trace of bygone springs
no care of sorrow or hurt
where the grief-stricken sleep in peace
Here go the dry leaves, here they go

Days of autumn are over
Now that they are gone, I have begun to think
Otherwise, as long as autumn lasted, my eyes remained
    wet with tears
The memory of spring was like the echo of a forgotten
    raga trembling in the heart
Spring, some ravishing girl in whose young body
a rush of pleasure surged
This lovely girl, where was she now?
Her absence in slow autumn moments was making her
    dearer, most precious
Autumn, like some stonehearted singer, stirred the
    tales of days past
Only one voice welled up on all sides
In the garden, signs of spring have been extinguished

The tulip flame of passion is no more
There is silence, but no peace
Neither a rose leaf nor trace of delirium
A regret in every eye
No more now those longings, nor bits of cloud
Sustained by the memory of spring
How far can we bear this grief?
In garden after garden, signs of spring have been
    extinguished
Alarmed, the birds of the garden
wantons of spring overtaken by autumn
have lost the use of their wings
They have lost their charm and manner
They pick at their wings and feathers needlessly
Bewildered by autumn, they wonder
how now to spend their life
In garden after garden, signs of spring have been
    extinguished

The moments of autumn are gone
Even when autumn was at ease, it was not quite so
    contented
Even when autumn was cruel, it was not quite so
    stonehearted
He who has sometime seen a winter evening pass
    before his eyes, he knows
If someone, sometime, has lived alone in a snow-
    covered mountain valley
then he certainly knows
how death plays with life's sad frame
Autumn, after all, was autumn—I was aware of
    destitution even in flowering springtime
But desires rustled within me in that state of indigence

Spring was, after all, spring—yet there was life even in autumn
But winter evening—
an icy indifference rules the whole world
I now yearn for the grief of straitened circumstances
There is no desire now that someone leap and touch the sky
and if any longing still lives in the heart
no one has the courage or wish to express it
for now winter evening spreads over the entire world

Translated from Urdu by Waqas Khwaja

Koël

Hearing the *koël*'s cries, my heart flutters with agitation,
every note of hers resounds with hurt and pleading.
How the poor dear wails, she is far from her beloved,
her pain cuts deep inside, perhaps she's been forsaken.
Such mournful songs, so full of sorrow, she sets the heart to
    shivering—
desolate, tormented as though crucified, she weeps in her
    vexation.
For a parted lover every tree is like the Mount of Moses!
Sometimes she sits in the wilderness and keens, or suddenly
    takes wing,
despoiled by fortune, distant from friends, altogether helpless—
alas, the poor girl's lamentations echo far and wide.
The naïve and guileless darling, distracted in her grief,
incessantly she cries and cries, "My beloved lies oblivious!
I suffer far from home, he is happy in his land.
Scanning roads and pathways, my eyes have lost their sight.
The river is a spate of sorrows, the shore seems far,
I will swim or else be swept across—that is, if God permits
(I offer thanks continually, I am indebted to His grace).
With all his charming talk, my love has my heart in thrall."
Constantly she cries, forever cheerless and grief-stricken,
"Come, love, show me your face, for you stay always hidden.
Don't be vain about your beauty, throw off, love, your pride!
From this impermanent world, dear heart, many loved ones
    have passed.

Not content, I wander restless, in my heart, this bleeding sore,
I raise a clamor, he replies with nothing—he is proud, so proud!
If others know the dear one better, I accept this as it is,
but how can I renounce him—when was this within my power?
I practice night and day the recitation of his name,
they desert, turn their face away—this is the custom of those we love."
Unswerving lovers are bruised and battered, crushed to bits,
yet love's path they do not leave, like Mansur they gladly mount the cross.
You too, my sweet, cry out, "I die! Death is all I wish.
I keep my promises—poet, write down these words!
My loyalty, his faithlessness, they are famed throughout the world.
The arbiter is in the heart, the universe, clemency itself."
Rich, poor, peasant, worker—
Janbaz, everyone says: Alas! She is ground to death by separation.

Translated from Seraiki by Azmat Ansari and Waqas Khwaja

Arrival of the Spring

To the first tree in the new house

Confidant of spring!
You, an innocent child
from some garden somewhere,
have come to me.
With such love
have I extended to you the hospitality
of a place in my courtyard.

Years shall pass.
Whenever spring comes,
you will scatter your songs
to the melody
of silken, flowering buds,
self-absorbed,
inscribe on the heart's tablet
perfumed works of art.

The thinking of the young,
conceit of the beautiful,
are both alike—
before their own image
all colors pale.

When spring arrives,
who knows where I will be?

The foot-track of destinations
is made up of twists and turns.
You, of course, will forget

my warm hands,
the dreams in my eyes.
I will not,
for I am, intrinsically, a mother.

Translated from Urdu by Asif Farrukhi

Even Today

I understand that I
am free today of all my debts,
have paid the price of each and every smile,
sincerely renounced devotion and constancy,
resolved to quit making mistakes.
Now even I am condemned to have a life,
and this heart that is willful, ignorant—
in today's age,
when sincerity, fidelity, and love too are official decrees,
when even tears have a price, scales everywhere to weigh and
    appraise—
this heart, even today,
longs for one spontaneous, uninhibited smile.

Translated from Urdu by Waqas Khwaja

Listen

Love,
you have no idea!
People often get upset
that at no stage or turn does my story
run through a dark lane—
for you, drawing every color from rays of light,
have assigned to each footprint of mine the rainbow.
There are neither shadows of lost dreams
nor whispering moments of despair,
for a sturdy tree
holds in its innumerable hands
a tender vine.
No failure haunts this pathway.
What kind of a journey is this that its narrative
is not to be found in the journey's clouds of dust?

Translated from Urdu by Waqas Khwaja

NASIR KAZMI

Ghazal: Bearing Hints of Bygone Days

Bearing hints of bygone days
Where did he come from, where did he go?
He was a strangely familiar stranger
He left me in a state of awe

Showing only his pearl-like face
Just playing for me a tuneful song
Like the evening star he came
And like a dream of dawn he left

In seasons of joy or days of sorrow
Eyes search for him everywhere all the time
Was he the rose's breath or the song of life
He came to inhabit my very heart

No more now the rising river of memories
No more the gloomy rain of empty hours
Just a brief ache in the heart
The deep wound has filled up and healed

The breath comes a little easier now
The course of the sky too is about to change
The night that was heavy has turned at last
The hard day is over

The capricious have but one goal
True lovers, a thousand paths
This alone is the difference between us
I moved on, he held back

Feet worn out, I stand in the way
Beckoning the days gone by
The caravan I traveled with
Has disappeared like the journey's dust

Even my blood has turned to water
Yet not an eyelash of the heartless shakes
The lament that rose from my heart last night
I wonder why it had no effect

He who would keep the tavern awake
Who used to put night's sleep to flight
What came into his heart today
He left for home at the twilight hour

That star of the night of separation
That dear friend, soul mate of mine
May his name be forever beloved
I heard last night he passed away

He with whom, hand on his shoulder,
You traveled to life's destinations
I don't know why with head hung low
He passed right through your lane today

That night's soundless traveler
That poet of yours, your own Nasir
I saw him go right up to your lane
Then I wonder which way he went

Translated from Urdu by Mehr Afshan Farooqi

Ghazal: He Is Charming but Not Perceptive

He is charming but not perceptive
my physician has no remedy for me

Many questions stir upon my tongue but
there is no worthy petition for me

My heart is anxious even in your presence
Contentment too is not suited to me

The days I once spent in your company
not even their charm is left to me

The heart and eye are passing through strange stages
I long for dawn, but no yearning for life is left in me

I fear my desire for you may not last
days have passed without even a hint of sadness for me

Translated from Urdu by Waqas Khwaja

Ghazal: When I Learned to Write

When I learned to write
first of all, I wrote your name

I am the absolute patience that
took upon itself the weight of trust

I am the exalted name to which
angels and jinns bowed in prayer

Why did you not take my hand
when my feet strayed from the path?

Whatever I have found is yours
whatever I have lost is also yours

I spent a lifetime without you
people will say that you were mine

O sender of the first rains
I thirsted for a glimpse of you

Translated from Urdu by Mehr Afshan Farooqi

A Gecko's Mind

A gecko's mind is embedded in our brain—
the spark of Abu Lahab, Father of Fire?
An ancient intelligence
a legacy of creeping, crawling things, they say
but one that, even today, is an unavoidable part of our brain
I am not such a worshiper of rhyme and meter
that caught between fear and devotion I stretch matters and say
it's only a story
I'll say what is generally claimed, that it's a legacy

∎

The sensible all call it the Reptilian Complex
although other organisms are located in the brain too

But that, and those nets of evolutionary marvels
from whose tangles it is difficult today to escape—
well, not in a thousand, but perhaps in a hundred thousand or
    a billion years
it will all be unraveled

∎

My subject today is the gecko's brain:
since I can find today no escape
from storms of devastation and terror in my own city and
    homeland

this strange, unruly prison house of aggression and infernal conjunctions
this hot, poisoned wind of tyranny and oppression
this proprietary lust

■

They say that all brutality humans exhibit comes from this
that, in the stages of evolution, a close connection exists also between
    man and many species of beast
There is no conclusive evidence as to whether humans are a separate
    species or part of the same chain
but, based on their logic, research, and experimentation, this deduction
    is inevitable
that I should live in these complex, expanding circles of reasoning
drink up the wine of the world's scientific creeds

This is not how it really is
They say that this malice, bewilderment, and hatred
this flaring up at the least excuse
this half-hidden, half-manifest evolving story of those very stages—
that person is not aware of creation's history who doesn't acknowledge this

■

So now, my question—
I don't care that it has been asked before, for my approach is original

■

When evolution has secured for us the honor of the best of creatures
so is it determined that in future ages this part of our brain will remain
    affianced to the devil's deceptions?
Today we are love and beauty
many virtuous qualities

within our reach and grasp, advance from excellence to excellence
Numberless mysteries are beginning to disclose themselves to us
that once lay hidden, veiled from consciousness
although even now there is no knowledge—just learning and information
But we are not bereft of the ability, the wisdom, to know

Thousands of fertile opportunities lie ahead
Whether they be destinations or pathways, they are before us

.

These awe-inspiring discoveries of genetics
this sweeping current of multidimensional breakthroughs every minute
this splicing of a hundred possibilities in sperm and egg—
the heat of these pursuits
so, will we then not find, over the next hundred thousand years or so,
    some means
by which we can disable in our brain, indeed expel from it every trace
    of the gecko's mind
and afterwards, from fuel of love and striving and high action, burn,
    eternally fortunate, such colorful lamps
that end the flames of Abu Lahab's primeval broil of contentiousness
and bestow upon man the grace to become human?

.

The beginning is the beginning and not the end that this journey
    between the two stretches out so long and wondrous—
no thought, idea, or thing within this changes

.

God is merciful. Why would He wish, dear heart,
that to the end Satan should remain thus attached to man?

That faith should never triumph over sin?
Why would He wish that some remain misguided to the end
who, upon dying, are sent straight to Hell?

.

If, as some say—
a thing that fascinates modern scholars,
although I still don't agree with them—
the origin is no origin and eternity no eternity
there never was a beginning and there will be no end
then there is no dispute over good and ill with anyone—
it is up to each to say whatever is in the heart
bubble, gecko, man, evolution, call it what you will.

Translated from Urdu by Khurram Khurshid and Waqas Khwaja

Orthography

Sovereign Master,

Pardon my speech impediment.

In attempting to extinguish the fire in which I burn again
after all these years,

all oceans and rivers of richly colored images have shrunk to
a narrow strait.

Immersing myself in them, appraising the outcome of my
diffident thoughts and expressions,

my practice of art becomes the disgrace of art,

and the beloved's cry from the cup of wisdom in numberless
taverns

turns out to be but self-indulgence.

I did not have the courage to tackle all directions—whatever
genre I pursued,

like the beloved, betrayed its promise.

When I rose to beg some signs and symbols from the skies,
that path, too, led to the street of self-conceit.

■

Pardon my speech impediment.

That treasure hoard of ancestors' pearls has my respect.

All those distinctive idioms that like benevolent clouds spread
over my age, refuge of those who pursue the fresh and new,

and are tall, grand emblems,

generating schools, imbued with a hundred virtues, obligatory
elements that command veneration, each a world unto itself—

not of gleaning from them but of mistakes in imitating them
am I afraid.
Those who rise by profiting from them are accomplished
beyond compare, beloved by all, marvelously fortunate.
But those stylists themselves too are most honorable.
Compared to their treasure troves, what are my sapless,
unaccomplished fictions—harvests of ignorance, strangers
to art and beauty!
Respectful, the mere warmth of their footprints on my
forehead a blessing, I pass by alone
and submit, in this rough, rude, tradition-less (that is, my
very own) language, my aspiration.

.

God, Almighty!
Grant me at least as many centuries more
that I may observe, read, reflect, write, accomplish something.
If there are rewards, I should achieve something worthy
of them.
No, I don't say that now, or at some future time, I should
earn a name for myself,
but it is possible, with your blessing, that in this world of
misdemeanors I may acquit myself blameless.
These centuries were but the start of the alphabet,
or bey aleph, without beginning at all.

.

I have not yet understood—
that which was my right and my duty and, from those who
come and go, may be an obligation, too—
how features of so many galaxies, distant realms,

beyond and visible,

and others also—how they form, survive, and circle constantly,

why the regulation of my life is limited only to the scale of
diurnal time,

why my understanding is confined only to those sparks of light
that crumble immediately as they form.

Sources also tell of nameless, dark, wall-less, door-less black holes.

They say that these collapsed stars have such a gravitational field

that it pulls in the very light that passes by—

and, what is exasperating, they speak of how all this relates
to me!

Asked what that relationship might be, they smile sometimes in
mockery, sometimes in helplessness.

These centuries were but the start of the alphabet.

■

As to love's consummation,

a state, perhaps, that may itself not be divisible—

mere suggestions left, whether it will disclose itself, and, if it
does so, what its nature will be,

whether it will come within our apprehension or forever remain
beyond reach.

And, regarding the pearl of understanding,

that unrewarding anxiety and incertitude, unacknowledged to
this day,

will it lead eventually to some splendorous signification, or will
the atmosphere of tumult and misfortune persist to the very
end of time?

Singularity, uniqueness, singularity!

That one particle of exceptional density whose other name,

its material form,

was rendered all energy—

even knowing this, it is beyond comprehension
what thing this was.

What is it, why did it stir to life, why does it keep expanding?

Will it ever reverse itself? If so, what is likely to bring this about?
   What shape would it take?

Singularity!

And in all this timeless time and spaceless space, how might my
   life be implicated?

For I, too, am a living individual, and because I am living, I
   must in some way be implicated—

yet in this incertitude or certainty, in this existence and life, I
   am blameless indeed as well.

By the legacy of Adam! I am unhappy with him, too.

These centuries were but the start of the alphabet.

■

A thought arose
that cried out loud:

Having come this far, you still desire your reward?

Henceforth too, then, you will be remembered as one who lusts
   after what you desire, accomplishment is not for you.

Orthography?

Taxonomies, galaxies, orbits, circles, holes, their mysterious
   powers of attraction, the consummation of love?

Now that the roses and thorns of some minor affairs, a surfeit
   of short-lived luxuries, occasional tears and pleasures have
   left you without wine and *saqi*,

your destitute brain longs for the privilege of understanding
   galactic secrets?

Fool, it is not within your power to vanquish the summit of
   desire!

Look at what is engraved in bold letters on the wall of Eternity!

It says the likes of you shall never have the wealth of reflection
    and tranquility—
lie rotting in the prison house of death and superfluity!

■

Sovereign Master!
God Almighty!

■

A thought arose, vexed this time:
Show some shame, at least, in the perverse desire for a new
    opportunity from the wasteland of ambition.
The sanguinary tales of the free-spirited, that striving of the
    eminent departed—
you don't have quite their stature, don't try to imitate them.
For the moment, acknowledge only this:
In orthography, too, were recorded the modulations of the art
    of elocution—
you have yet not learnt the melody of the first word.
Life on this piece of earth remains dominant in all your
    themes—
a life that is transient.
Thousands of centuries pass, and still it is a brief and unfinished
    tale.
And yet willful arrogance sparks in you the obsession to prove
that something of the immortal there is in you.

■

It was enough for you to attach yourself to life's buried and
    unburied treasures—

words, lusts, campaigns, logic, peace, beauty and love, superstitions,
revelation, invention,
all those constraints, those crutches, all those metaphors, sad and
joyous,
now prosperous, now devastated—
among them, in your struggle for and delusion of immortality,
nourish yourself on mere morsels of fame and respect.

■

Now you are exceeding yourself,
walking the sky from your place on earth!
Well.
But don't gorge yourself on more than you can digest—
let your ardor and restlessness sink to the bottom of your brain.
If the grief of self-indulgence and obscurity takes hold—this is
difficult, but you can at least try—
those moments that are left you, dedicate them to the peace or the
madness that circulates within them.
Who knows what you may gain if the indifferent one disputes
and reasons!
Who knows what he may conceal or disclose?
Singularity, it is an enigma,
a mysterious flow,
into which, according to experts of both worlds, you too will be
absorbed—
perhaps the movement of a single neutron will make you one
with it.
If it exists,
in whatever form or body,
it may perhaps fulfill its own goals through you.

■

O plain speech and wisdom, prosper, prosper, prosper!

.

The thought turned away,
but turned back again, and this time it neither cried nor spoke in
    vexation but most calmly remarked,
You have no monopoly over this striving, this conversation,
or over any impatient stream of longing born of some fount of
    oneness.
Many, mute and eloquent, have come parched with thirst, many
    more will come—
if you drink up every drop, how will they slake their thirst?
But O man of the world, what fleeting vision will these curtains of
    self-deluding comfort part to offer your active understanding?
You are concerned only about prolonging your own life,
in the midst of fatigue and weariness you seek only your own
    invigoration.

.

If you are truly burning with ambition, then look also at those
    flames
that fire the heart of curiosity and exploration generation after
    generation.
Who knows what customs and precepts, ancient and illustrious,
world-reigning,
shatter immediately, helpless and delighted, at the first jolt of a new
    insight, experiment, or discovery?
And how many wayward, willful, and isolating worries and problems
    still remain, even in the face of this era's quickened assault?
Even in such conditions, no one claims that this assembly of the
    world's sages, much like Solomon's legions, has the means to
    overcome them—

new targets within old perplexities, this period's customs and
    practices, exempt from laws, are stages of discontinuity
that are at times autonomous, at others a part of regulation.
For instance, propagation
and all its manifestations—
are they merely billows without a cause,
unregulated elements of the sea of space?
Or some lovers of the shore after their own kind and
    fashion?
What are they? Are they headed somewhere or only hurtling
    along without destination?
Singularity. Oneness.
That soul of substance: matter, energy—
why only that?
Is there some other reality, a sign from the invisible, manifest?
No one knows what its mysteries are—
its negations and affirmations lie only in the flow of its own
    nurturing, passions, and ruminations.
But this speculation persists in its freshness:
Whatever it is, it is some saga of incompletion or of ecstasy!
You should know only this, from the time it began, if it exists at
    all, it exists only for itself, or it belongs to everyone.
Never before did it belong to just one, nor will it ever.

Come, understand that your life, afflicted or pleasant, however
    it may be, from first to last belongs to it.

What is often said, embrace it: please your heart and, when the
    time comes, die!

Nor abandoning your heat of reflection and doubt, and curiosity's
    similar unruly, crude,
whirling sparks in the rose garden of art

(much reviled in the smug assembly of the certain),

breaking up those pretty flowerbeds prepared with such love
and labor,

cause the flowers of their enchanting contentment to be set
aflame,

nor melt away your delicate corporeal form,

nor, in your mind, which is already tiring, get knocked around
from door to door.

■

If you do get another six or seven centuries, how will it help?

It will be the same story,

only this, isn't it, that whatever it is now, it may be just a little
bit different?

But all past destinations themselves suggest

(if you retrace your steps and then come back)—they show
you the writing on each particle of dust along the way,

that however many obstacles you cross, still others will
lie ahead.

■

Those in whom you have faith, they themselves admit that
this excess of heat will last yet for another six, seven million
years or more.

Let this be for those who come after: they, too, have to show
up and display their cleverness—

but how long will you and all the other self-absorbed sages
remain oblivious to this?

How much further can we take you now?

Singularity. Oneness.

That soul of substance: matter, energy—

those in whom you have faith, they themselves say that it will
    once more converge to a point,
concentrating and absorbing all its forces,
seize all your galaxies, planets, and perverse systems,
eras and eons, places and infinite spaces.
That which started the journey with a bang,
with a bang it will return.

Turn whatever page of wisdom you will,
you will remain bereft of knowledge to the end.
Doomsday, too, must come.

■

It may again stir to life after this, and who knows what it
    may become!
It—or something, someone, greater than itself—may amuse itself
    with who knows what exceptional patterns and paradigms for
    new games—
these paradisal thoughts, obsolete or fresh,
the exigency and prerogative to disclose or to conceal—
what will it be called at that time?
Only he who discovers it may tell.

■

Sovereign Master!
Thought, though a pleasant conversationalist, unsatisfying
    ultimately, turned out to be an adversary of aspiration—
a little I have understood; still, much I have not.
Show me, in my own mirrors, the image of becoming.
Grant me a few centuries, after all, in which I may learn all the
    characters and words—

from them I need to fashion a language of my own, an interpretation
   of this world and the universe.
Whatever the wise have bequeathed me, and whatever else they
   will give, I accept, but
the world of questions that is in my heart—it may be connected
   with the past, present, and future, yet still
it is fixed in my own commitment and strife—
it is mad.
But its madness, too, is the story of my limitless quest for you.

■

These centuries were but the beginning of the alphabet.

Translated from Urdu by Waqas Khwaja

HABIB JALIB

Code

The flame of which burns only in palaces
Lights only a few on the road to happiness
That flourishes in every shade of expedience
    Such a code of life, such dawn without light
    I do not recognize, I do not accept

I am not cowed by the hangman's deck
I too am Mansur, go tell this to the enemy
Why try to scare me with prison walls
    The act of injustice, the night of ignorance
    I do not recognize, I do not accept

Flowers have begun to bloom, you say it
Wine begins to flow again for lovers, you say it
The gashed hearts are stitched up again, you say it
    This open lie, this insult to the mind
    I do not recognize, I do not accept

You have plundered our peace and quiet for centuries
Your blandishments will no longer work on us
How can I call you a friend and well-wisher
    You are no friend—one may see this or not
    I do not agree, I do not accept

Translated from Urdu by Waqas Khwaja

Political Advisor

This is what I said to him

> These that are a hundred million
> Are the distillation of foolishness
> Their thinking is in deep sleep
> Every ray of hope
> Sunk irretrievably in darkness
> It is true
> They are no longer alive
> They are unenlightened people
> Diseased for life
> And you possess
> The cure for their disease

This is what I said to him

> You are the Divine light
> Wise, sagacious
> The nation is wholly behind you
> Your existence alone
> Guarantees its salvation
> You are the moon of a new dawn
> After you, unremitting night
> The few that speak up
> Are all troublemakers
> Pull out their tongues
> Squeeze their windpipes

This is what I said to him

    Those who fancied their eloquence

    Those talkative ones, are silenced

    The land is in peace

    An extraordinary difference

    Between the past and present

    People under your rule

    Are confined at their own expense

    And he alone is distinguished

    Who lies prone at your doorstep

    He who asks for refuge

    Is freely forgiven

This is what I said to him

    Every minister, every ambassador

    Is a peerless counselor

    Wah, how remarkable!

    By your supreme intelligence

    Your choice is par excellence

    The State's officers are awake

    The masses in deep slumber

    And this, your minister

    Issues such statements

    That those who read them

    Marvel at their wisdom

This is what I said to him

    China, of course, is our friend

    Our life for it, if need be

    But the system they have

    Don't ever think of going there

    Wish it well from afar

    These hundred million asses

Whom we call the masses
Should they dream of ruling us?
You are "faith," they, "error"
I pray for only this
That you, my President, should rule forever

This is what I said to him

Translated from Urdu by Waqas Khwaja

Everyone Else Forgot How to Write the Word of Truth

Everyone else forgot how to write the word of truth
It was left to me to write of dissent and disobedience

Much advised not to write of injustice as injustice
I have not learned, my dear, to write by permission or license

I have the desire to seek neither reward nor praise
It is merely a habit to write on behalf of the forgotten masses

Since I never wrote a paean even forgetfully for the king
Perhaps this is one virtue that has taught me how to write

What greater praise can I have than this
That the affluent are unhappy at what I write

Faced with the calamity of fortune I quite forgot
To write of cypress-like beauties as the apocalypse of youth

Whatever the king's companions may say Jalib
Maintain this color of yours, and, just as you do, write

Translated from Urdu by Waqas Khwaja

MUNIR NIAZI

Cry of the Desert

Pitch-dark all around
heavy, rolling clouds—
She says, "Who?"
I say, "I"—
"Open this heavy door,
let me come inside"—
After this, a lingering quiet
and the roar of hurtling winds

Translated from Urdu by Alka Roy

I Always Wait Too Long

I wait too long to do anything
to say what needs to be said, to make good a promise
to call out to someone or urge someone back
I wait too long

to help someone, to reassure a friend
or go down timeworn paths to reach someone
I wait too long

to find solace in strolling through changing seasons
to remember someone, to forget someone else
I wait too long

to save a dying person from some grief
tell them that the truth was something else
I always wait too long

Translated from Urdu by Alka Roy

Love Will Not Happen Now

Stars that glint
in awestruck eyes
trysts in the splendor
of rain and clouds—
not now, but in desolate hours
of the melancholy heart,
love will not happen now
but later
when these days have passed.
It will happen in remembering them.

Translated from Urdu by Alka Roy

MUSTAFA ZAIDI

Meet Me for the Last Time

Meet me for the last time so that burning hearts
may turn to ashes and make no more demands,
that the torn vow is not sewn up nor the wound of desire bloom,
breathing remain steady, not even the candle's flame endure,
just so much conversation that passing moments may come and
    count the words,
if hope raises its eyelids, its eyes be blotted out.

This time there is no expectation that this tryst
will lead to another—
no time now for passion or frenzy, for parables and storytelling,
no time for renewal of love or for complaints.
In the city of mishaps the merchandise of words is lost.
If one must mourn now, how can one shape one's lament?
Until today I shared with you many ties of nerve and sinew,
when tomorrow starts, what will that relationship be called?

Never again will your cheek and face glow, come!
Doors and walls are mournful at this time of parting, come!
Never again will we be, nor pledges, nor denials—come!

Meet me one last time.

Translated from Urdu by Amritjit Singh and Waqas Khwaja

Come, my people, proceed to the mountain of revelation!

How long will you continue to be confounded by new gods?
You must be tired of revelry in dens of desolation.
Days, everywhere, decline in the same manner—
in every city people go about like shades,
harboring a secret fear in their hearts,
carrying on their backs caskets of their own haunting,
in self-mortification, in the shame of public places.
You too are a part of the crowd's isolation,

you too a wandering seeker, looking toward the skies.

Consider, yourself, what you received from each and every door,
whether or not your supplication was successful.
Who were they that persecuted you in your own streets?
In the wilderness of indigence, where did day break or dusk fall?
Who disturbed the sleeping harbingers of sorrow?
Who explained to you matters of discovering pleasure in pain?
Who brought you to the travails of love?

Where will you go now—what is native, and what foreign, land?
Everywhere signs point in the same direction,
one's voice is scattered among other voices,
one's pride is vexed, always on guard.
Only when consumed in flames does one discover the ashes of feeling,

in the fire of time find the smoke of fleeting moments.
Paths lose themselves continually in silences,

torches travel toward the wind on their own.

How much longer, hashish nights of storytelling and incantation?
The lust for sex, and the evening of promise, how much longer?
How can the body's wall sustain the mind?
How much longer can the bedchamber support the weight of pain?
For eyes that have been so long deprived of sleep,
how much longer the drugged cheek and heavy eyelash?
How many more days will the body's thirst call you

to song and flirtation, to vain and trifling graces?

All night long lamps in shops stay lit,
while the heart, that barren island, remains plunged in darkness.
But in every corner of this island,
the self's chapter of talismans remains open.
Within one's self are found the ruins of one's debasement,
and within one's self the mountain of revelation.
Only in this mountain's embrace is redemption possible,
otherwise, man remains encircled by mere objects,
until from them, too, he turns his eyes

toward his faith, toward his God.
Come, my people, proceed to the Mount of the Call.

Translated from Urdu by Amritjit Singh and Waqas Khwaja

Siege

My enemy has sent this message
that his forces have surrounded me.
On every tower and minaret of the city's wall
his soldiers stand with bows ready.

That electric power has been shut off
whose heat used to stir a fire in this body of clay,
dynamite planted in the waters
of the stream that once flowed toward my street.

All talkative mouths now suffer broken bones,
all rebels are consigned to the gallows.

All sufis and renunciants, all elders and imams,
in hopes of favor frequent the hall of the social elite.
To take their oaths of allegiance, the guardians of law
like hunched supplicants sit along the way.

You sang praises of the pride of writers and poets,
but those stars of talent's sky are now arrayed before you:
at one signal from a royal courtier these beggars of discourse
abase themselves in hordes before your very eyes.

Just look at the worldly assets of these *qalandars* of faith;
who is beside you, look about and around!

This, then, is the condition, if you wish to preserve your life:
put away your tablets and pens in the field of gallows,
otherwise, this time, the target for the archers
will be none but you—so leave your self-respect by the wayside.

Seeing this stipulation drawn, I asked the envoy,
Is he not aware of the lessons of history?
When night martyrs some flaming, glorious sun,
morning sculpts another one for the dawn.

So this is my answer to my foe:
I have neither desire for favor nor fear of consequence.
He takes great pride in the might of the sword.
He has no idea of the pen's eminence.

My pen is not this burglar's covetous hand
who cuts a hole in the roof of his own home.
My pen is no companion of this midnight thief
who casts a noose on houses plunged in darkness.

My pen does not extol that preacher
who keeps a register of his devotions.
My pen is not the scales of the judge
who wears a double mask upon his face.

My pen is a trust from my people,
my pen is the tribunal of my conscience.
That is why, whatever I wrote, it was with my soul's eloquence—
that is why the bow bends with such ease, my tongue straight as
    an arrow.

Whether I am cut down or remain secure, I believe
that someone at last will break this siege.

By my life's allotted afflictions I swear
my pen's journey will not end in despair.

If love's disposition has not experienced helplessness,
then high status is blindness and the measuring of shadows.

Translated from Urdu by Waqas Khwaja

Why Should We Sell Our Dreams?

We maintained the ascetic's way
but were never so needy
as to sell our dreams.
We walked around carrying our wounds in our eyes,
but when were we ever two-faced vendors in the marketplace?
Our hands were empty,
but never like this
that we hawked
our despoiled condition
with fireflies of words,
calling out in streets:
"Dreams for sale! Dreams!"
O people!
When were we so abject?
Why should we sell our dreams,
in longing for which
we had lost even our eyes?
Out of love for
and devotion to which
we had snuffed the candles of all temptations?

True, we, the voiceless,
are deprived of roof, and terrace, and door.
Very well, ill-fated, we are without accomplishment or skill.
But why should we sell the fables of our skies
and the moon and stars of our earth?
Bidding buyers,

you have brought your heaps of paper,
your dirhams and dinars from the marketplace of lust!
You bring such snares every time—
but why should we sell to you our peacock words,
the ruddy shelduck of our blood?
Our dreams may be inconsequential,
unfulfilled,
but they are dreams of the heart-stricken,
not the dreams of Zuleikha, Potiphar's wife,
that cast aspersions on the Josephs of their desire,
nor the dreams of the worthies of Egypt
whose interpretation prison inmates must provide,
nor are they the dreams of tyrants
who bring God's unprotected creatures to the gallows,
nor the dreams of plunderers
who put to sword the dreams of others.
Our dreams are dreams of the pure of heart,
dreams of change and good fortune—
dreams of forsaken doors,
dreams of besieged voices.
And why should we trade this rare wealth?
Why should we sell our dreams?

Translated from Urdu by Waqas Khwaja

ZAFAR IQBAL

Ghazal: The Flower that Bloomed Beneath the Ground Is in My Heart

The flower that bloomed beneath the ground is in my heart
Ever since he retreated behind the veil, he lives within my heart

He that these fools have just expelled from the city
That flame, the color of lips, is here within my heart

Life's path is lit a little by the blisters on my bare feet
And a small light from faith's candle burns within my heart

The hundred moons of Solomon are nothing to me
The precious jewel of Bilquis's lips lies within my heart

The world will long for these trembling rays of light
Until the time this luminous moon shines within my heart

Where is it to be found, the spell of this complex face?
Though a hundred beautiful pictures exist within my heart

Specters of some dream flit before my eyes
Some misty memory somewhere I have within my heart

I am not attached only to the flagstone at time's door
A waxen image also lives within my heart

I go around showing this ace to the inept,
which splendor is it, otherwise, that is not within my heart?

Translated from Urdu by Waqas Khwaja

Ghazal: Time Will Tell You One Day What I Am

Time will tell you one day what I am
Fire, ashes, the sun, or a mere particle

My heart's wound may not match your flowering garden
But I too carry around a little treasure with me

You are imprinted on the walls of my soul
Don't hide your face from me—I am your veil

Preserving in my eyes the image of some difficult valley
I burn, prostrate, in the desert of incapacity

All day long a sheet is stretched across feeling
When evening falls, I weep like dew

A wave comes and obliterates my image
I should drown, so long have I been at the water's lip

Translated from Urdu by Waqas Khwaja

Ghazal: Who Gave the *Jhoomar* of Pale Leaves to Dust's Forehead?

Who gave the *jhoomar* of pale leaves to dust's forehead?
From whose momentary self-revelation did dry wildernesses
    become green?

Small fairies remained huddled in their tiny enchanted palaces
    until the evening
Until the evening, flowers of snow continued to fall in the valley
    of Kaf

Perhaps once again this rain-soaked darkness will gleam
Perhaps once again the black princess of thick clouds will break
    into laughter

Again, like a lost soul, the breeze, on slow feet
has come to toss a pebble in the pool of memory

Sunflower of beauty's skies, sister of my heart
where are you? My fingers are tired—come plant your lips on them

Translated from Urdu by Waqas Khwaja

Anthem

Our country is awake, awake our native land!
Tyranny will end, the tyrant will be driven from our home.
Our country is awake!
Long have we borne the oppressor,
to outsiders have paid tribute—
tyranny has laid waste our prospering homeland.
Our country is awake!
Once our authority stretched as far as Kabul—
that was one age, this is another.
Now the sickle has slashed cruelty and injustice at the root.
Our country is awake!
The moon of art and culture we once set
with diamonds and precious stones,
kept thriving the arts, crafts, and industry—
our homeland, a bejeweled masterwork.
Our country is awake!
When autumn's breeze turned pale the delicate flowers,
when we awoke to our country's condition,
the land blossomed with revolution's fire.
Our country is awake!

Translated from Kashmiri by Saleem Kamili

Kashmir Is a Lion

We remember the massacre at Karbala,
horrors and atrocities do not frighten us—
we are ever ready to offer up our lives for honor and justice,
we have faith that we will uproot evil and oppression.
We respect and revere knowledge,
we have no use for rogues and scoundrels.

The outsiders ruling Kashmir gather up the *pharons* of its open fields.
We smote our own necks.
To sleep is in the nature of those who feed upon the dandelion
("Sleep is the sister of death," the wise have said),
but Kashmir is a sleeping lion.
Even in sleep, the lion keeps an eye open.

Translated from Kashmiri by Saleem Kamili

Taos! It is impossible to forget those days—
how can one not recall the year '48?
I feel the calendar has reversed itself,
and the year has become '84.
I remember it like the meal I ate last night, or like my mother's milk.
When the UN commission arrived in Kashmir,
in high schools and colleges everywhere
young men proclaimed:
"Freedom is our birthright!
We will run the Indian army out all on our own!
Tyrants, when will you hear our cry?"
But those assassins sent heartless jackals.
College students, as tender as budding flowers,
were beaten senseless by those cutthroats,
pummeled by the butts of guns and rifles.
Half dead already under the tyrant's blows
many passed out, cruelly wounded—
but their hearts swelled with undiminished zeal.
The murderers snatched at and tore our blood-stained garments,
packed us into trucks, as if we were four-legged animals,
and took us with our sorrows to the prison.
They started scheming to silence us,
but we cried only, "We are free!"
Those who recovered consciousness shouted, "Zindabad!"
That scene is still before my eyes.
I lay naked, helpless with injuries,
until, a long while later, I was revived by an angel.

I heard a familiar voice—
that of my friend, who was also injured.
Wiping away the blood, Hajni Sahib said,
"My son, Umlala! Oh, Shameema!
Don't lose heart! This is all just *bismillah*.
Tyranny and repression won't last forever—
remember all that our prophet endured!"

Translated from Kashmiri by Saleem Kamili

Half Poem

I keep practicing my obsession.
Who knows when that manly moment may arrive
that will tear open the shirtfront of this ordinary, civilized poem
and disclose words of naked-eyed truth?
Tears, breaking on the shore of vacant eyes,
water the soil of darkness.
Any remedy? The race of mediocrities—
sever me from the legacy of its ages!
The heart says,
Come, on the highest peak of danger
let's dance that life-disrobing dance
the sight of which drives the whole world mad,
stirs up eyes that have slept for centuries within the blood
and, in the interval of a spark, this half poem completes itself.

Translated from Urdu by Waqas Khwaja

Romance of Imagination

No! Keep to yourself your teardrop
that contains the perspective of eternity—
filtered through it, all distances
all light, the whole air, are cleansed.
The painter of light has painted a scene
of cross and gallows and dry watercourse.
Zapata, Che Guevara, and Mao
are not defeated in defeat—
those who assaulted the windmills
will forever keep returning.
What can be done? When this old water bag is repaired
it still drips from the stitches.
The fault lies with the needle-worker—
or is it with the thread spun from sunlight on the spinning wheel?
It is said that the blind singer has received an intimation
of excellence, but
with the striking bow he must
first break a hundred thousand *sarangi* strings.

Translated from Urdu by Waqas Khwaja

The Waterwheel Turns

Where the sun goes down every day,
in some land, in that region,
when philosophies arrived as migrants, first the teacher's wisdom
disclosed itself.
The foundation of the potential-for-growth culture was laid
centered on interest and world trade.
The standard-bearers of this singular vision acquired an empire
on which the sun never set.
In the cloth of its logic were wrapped
inquiry, analysis, and discovery.
Following the prince of wisdom, it
drew lines of color, race, language,
and geography, in the service of necessity,
and parceled out these little pieces,
occupied the passage and extremity of every sea.
My good man! What do you think,
History is some slut?
A coach hitched by the sultan's door?
Or the declensions of grammar?
And are these teeming millions bullocks bound
in the yoke of the world?
What should I say! I am not
some rebel from the past century.
How should I go about interpreting life
from the perspective of sex and economics, ego or élan vital?
I am an ascetic possessed
who must, in the river that has wept itself dry,

let fall another teardrop.

One day, in the villages and towns that God has settled,

everything must turn upside down.

Have you not seen?

Yesterday, there, the great day of audacity

trounced the self-evident nature of God Almighty's plans and powers.

Events are happening—

the world's destiny is about to be rewritten.

Perhaps it is nearing time for the banquet of joy,

the term of despair is about to be reduced.

Look at the season of love's unveiling—

just look at the word of revelation written on the prophetic tablet
   of tomorrow.

Translated from Urdu by Waqas Khwaja

Ghazal: The Luster of a Pearl Is Something Else

The luster of a pearl is something else
The sparkle of eyes, something else

The depth of the sea is a reality
The heart of a poet, something else

The cooing of a dove is music
The roar of cannons, something else

Clouds change color at twilight
The nuclear cloud is something else

What is in the heart is on the lips as well
The poet's demeanor is something else

The body is a cage for the soul
A cage for the cage, something else

Look at the bloodstains and weep
Whose blood this is, something else

Pure gold shines bright
A smiling face is something else

Gold is good, and so is silver
The heart is something else

Hope is support enough, Tanveer
The fear of pain, something else

Translated from the Sindhi by Asif Farrukhi and
Shah Mohammed Pirzada

Ghazal: Nobody Knows to Whom We Belong

Nobody knows to whom we belong—
everybody is somebody's very own

What is the world? Nothing much to think about!
We continue nonetheless to give out love

Where Adam and Eve were,
we, too, are standing there

We are like leaves and buds—
we decay and sprout again

The world keeps looking
and we keep moving on

Translated from the Sindhi by Asif Farrukhi and
Shah Mohammed Pirzada

Writing a Poem

Writing a poem
is like catching butterflies
or plucking a rose
or caressing the face
of a beautiful girl
as if I am holding
lightning in my hands
or in my clenched fists
imprisoning
the whirlwind

Translated from the Sindhi by Asif Farrukhi and
Shah Mohammed Pirzada

Compromise

Silky and snug chador of compromise
I have woven this chador over many years
No flowers or shrubs of truth anywhere
Not a single stitch of any falsehood

Even with this I will cover my body
With this you, too, will be content
You will be neither happy nor melancholy

Stretched above us, it will make a home
If we spread it out, the courtyard will bloom
If we raise it, a curtain will fall

Translated from Urdu by Waqas Khwaja

Evening's First Star

When a strong gust of wind,
struck by some thought, passed by,
when the face of the burning sun
was wrapped in an azure scarf,
when the breast of dry land
stirred with the dew of breath,
that evening we were all together.

He who laughed and looked at us,
he was our first friend—
the evening star,
who had, perhaps, for the two of us
appeared a little early.

When that resplendent room
was hazy with cigarette smoke,
when the wormwood of liquor
had sweetened everyone's speech,
every anxiety had its own destination,
every reverie its own course,
that night we were all together.

What a stir there was!
I, engrossed in civilities,
you, delighting in revelry.
The subject on which
we spoke and reflected

was the changing world.
Some talk there was of weather and climate.

When the smoke in the room
got in everybody's eyes,
I opened up the window,
you pulled back the curtain.
He that looked at us with sorrow
was again that first friend of ours—
the evening star,
who, perhaps, for the two of us
that night was up till the crack of dawn.
Evening's first star.

Translated from Urdu by Waqas Khwaja

ATA SHAD

Lament of the Merchants of Hope

This is what the heart says,
I am neither morning nor evening,
I am neither true dawn nor twilight.
What rainbow, what clouds, what morning breeze?
What planet Earth?
How long must a fakir beg for alms!
The heart feels and understands,
desire is like a tired traveler
without destination.
We have heard that night will come.
They say that a certain day will dawn.
Who knows the night, and who the day?
Both are dead.
Clouds of joy and sorrow range above me,
love's autumn is springtime to me.
I tie the knot of hope—He leads me to despair.
The rituals of enmity and friendship last but forty days.
In the mirror of sleep, the whole world has become a marketplace,
and in this marketplace
joys begin to go soft and stale from the very start.
The fertile valley sparkles like pearls—
eyes are blind to it, the ears turn deaf.
It reveals itself in a flash of lightning and glows like burnished gold.
What rainbow, what clouds, what morning breeze!
What planet Earth!
And in this marketplace,
you and I are sold,

we all are sold—
and the heart, like a beggar,
endures the rebuff.
Like a speechless traveler, desire plods on
without destination.

Translated from Balochi by Azmat Ansari and Waqas Khwaja

The Road of Memory

Come, where are you, profound and learned collections of my thoughts?
   Where?
My eyes pine to see you!
Tears weave a thread of pearls, no less than the latticed window of my
   memories.
This is the way I compete with the clouds.
The day like fire and twilight like burning embers rain on my heart—
I fight against my thoughts like a madman.
I am not Shah Murid that I can enlist a pigeon from holy Mecca as my
   messenger,
I am not Jam Durrak that the rainbow itself asks after my well-being,
I am not crazy for a glimpse of your glory, like Mast Tawakali.
I have no memory of Hani, Sammo, or Sangeen.
You are that dream of an expired night I have forgotten—
or the opening line of a love poem that flits through the mind and is
   gone—
or music of the morning breeze that can only be felt, not seen.
You are the firefly that glimmers in the night and then vanishes—
or the clap of lightning? I do not know!
Or the night's new moon that has just emerged but cannot be seen,
or the false dawn, obscured by clouds and rain,
or a mullah's faith (that no one knows what it is)?
Or are you waiting for God, to see when He might show Himself?
Or are you that dream of God whose time of fulfillment is not known?
Or are you, like Abraham's father, a worshiper of idols?
Or are you the secret tears of a lover?
Come, where is that place where in my desolation I may find some rest?

When will my eyes be cooled by your sight?

When will my tears relent and let the clouds shield me with their shade?

My heart boils in the perpetual fire of this world.

I do not know my path or my destination—

I am lost on the slopes of this earthly world.

How long must I sustain my grieving heart with wine?

How long must I pine for a soothing glimpse of my beloved?

How long must I yearn for the dark tresses of women with sleep-heavy eyes

and for the fragrance that spreads when they shake their *dupattas*?

Where are you, profound and learned volumes of my thoughts?

Come, where is the beloved of my imagination?

Come, where is that place where in my desolation I may find some rest?

When will my eyes be cooled by your sight?

Translated from Balochi by Azmat Ansari and Waqas Khwaja

Power and Powerlessness

Dear God! Dear God!
Where is that world,
that sky, that earth,
that night and that morning,
those flowering stars and that majestic moon?
Where is that wine and those colorful fancies bathed in wine,
that best, most pleasant of seasons,
the world that is my resting place, but is physically separated from
    my body,
where my sinless soul alarms and bewilders the tribe of angels—
the world that is far from hell's punishment
for the deliberate sins of my old age,
where my countless unfulfilled desires equal the price of heaven?
In the market of sorrow and grief,
where neither I nor my home exist?
I have traveled long to reach my place of rest
but to this moment I have not found it.
Where is it? Where?
That earth, that sky,
that world!
Dear God! Dear God!
It is here!
Myself. I am a crumbling ruin of signs,
a deep ocean of dreams seeking salvation in the hereafter,
a churning vortex of bloodstained memories.
In the flow of time, in the sweeping winds and storms of the heart,
    who knows the walls of the ocean's waves?

Which way should I turn?
I will go down with the waters!
Where is that world?
Dear God, where is that world?

Translated from Balochi by Azmat Ansari and Waqas Khwaja

Traveler

Traveler,
step into my heart—
the earth is burning.
Why do you turn your face from one who gave you sanctuary?
Are you sure you understand what you are doing?
Despite our eyes, we are blind,
the heart is far removed.

I have been wringing my hands at what I have discovered
    of the world,
your bitter smiles.
The pain you have caused me is a reproach to life,
this pain will live forever in my heart.
We all await the dawn of a new morning.
Thoughts of your love spread above me like the shade
    of clouds,
the image of the destination is far from my mind.
I burn in a fire of thorns.
Where are they who no longer desire the world?
You are the embodiment of the pain of separation—
I am lost in thoughts of you.
Come, see the bier of my delirious fancies,
accept the favors of your brothers—
let me carry the weight of hopeless dreams from centuries
    past,
let me assume the burden of waiting.
The grave is narrow, dark, oppressive—

all that is left of luminous fancies.
Traveler,
step into my heart.
The whole earth is on fire.

Translated from Balochi by Azmat Ansari and Waqas Khwaja

In the Hour of Death

The eye remains open in the throes of death, and silence reigns.
This state has its own language, whether we admit it or not—
Eyes are needed to perceive it, ears to hear it.
The old generation witnessed a fearsome revolution, and yet this
    too is a time of adversity—
the hour of death.
The dying man sees, although his eyes have no light.
He is deaf, but his ears are listening—
there is a soul but no life.
See hatred and love and indifference disengage from the corpse,
the soul's agonized cries have shaken the entire world,
your ears are deaf, and my tongue mute.
How can your borrowed tongue be trusted?
I am like earth's shuddering rumble during an earthquake.
You are content only in this, that you have vanquished forts with
    sword and spear,
but I pine for my heritage and my motherland.
Born of Adam, I am the rightful heir to love and affection.
It is true that your success has wounded and subdued me.
You are pleased that your persecution and injustice
have killed a son,
and he, the son of freedom.
There is another son,
one who is the star of the motherland's eyes, the fulfillment of its
    heart's desire,
the hope of humanity's future,
the wish for perpetual happiness come true.

This son is the spirit of friendship; he is love's hope for tomorrow,
good tidings of the defeat of doom.
You cannot kill life's ideas by plucking a flower
nor, in this way, prevent the diffusion of its scent.
If you wish to destroy me, kill my soul first,
If my death is your desire, first hang love's hopes on the gallows,
and if you wish to annihilate me, first tear out the beams of the
    dwelling place of thought.
Strike down knowledge with an arrow—
I will not end with death.
I am love, I will not vanish.
My footprints will endure until the end of time—
as long as this world exists, the line of my blood will shine.
If I die, you die,
if you live, I live.
The eye remains open in the throes of death, and silence reigns.
This state has its own language, whether we admit it or not—
yet eyes are needed to perceive it, and ears to hear it.
The old generation witnessed a fearsome revolution, and yet this
    too is a time of adversity—
the hour of death!

Translated from Balochi by Azmat Ansari and Waqas Khwaja

KISHWAR NAHEED

Counterclockwise

Even if my eyes were to become the soles of your feet,
this fear would not leave you,
that though I am not able to see,
I can still perceive words and physical forms
like a fragrance.

Even if, to secure myself,
I would rub my nose off my face
in your presence,
this fear would not leave you,
that though I no longer have a sense of smell,
I am still able to speak.

Even if my lips,
singing praises of your worldly might,
became dry and soulless,
this fear would not leave you,
that though I have been rendered speechless,
I can still walk.

Even after binding me in the fetters of marriage vows,
of shame and modesty,
paralyzing me completely,
this fear would not leave you,
that though I am unable to walk,
I can still use my mind to think.

Fear of my freedom, my instinct for survival,
dread of my ability to think—
what strange specters occupy your thoughts?

Translated from Urdu by Yasmeen Hameed

Grass Is Just Like Me

Grass, too, is like me—
only by spreading itself under the feet does it attain
its life's wish.
Damp, what does it signify?
Chafing embarrassment?
Or passion's fire?

Grass, too, is like me—
just when it is able to lift its head
the mower arrives,
frenzied, to make it soft as velvet
and even it out.

So you toil
at leveling woman as well.
Neither the earth's urge to bloom,
nor woman's, dies.

If you ask me, that idea of cutting
a path was right.
Those who cannot stand the impairment
of a defeated spirit
become a patch of earth
and prepare a path for the strong—

they are husks of straw,
not grass.

Grass is just like me.

Translated from Urdu by Waqas Khwaja

Nightmare

The goat awaits slaughter
and I, the dawn,
for each day on the office desk I am slain.
This is my price
for the lies told.
Like fresh graves, faces heavy with powder
come to visit me—
in the cemetery of minds, only such adornments
are befitting.
My country and I were born at the same time,
but we both lost our ability to see in our childhood.
I have not seen bread.
I shape it in my mind and imagine myself eating it.
Many of my peers see it only in their dreams.
Women in my country
pray at the sight of the new moon
and save the remaining prayers
for the next sighting.
Even after affixing their thumbprint on the permission for a
      second marriage
they offer their prayers when they see the new moon,
perhaps to improve the afterlife for deceitful ones like us.
We boast of our military courage
and flies keep assaulting us.
We consider swords taller than ourselves as our ancestors
and wear their color on our tongues.

Those who pass their lives in rust-worn tongues and times are
office clerks.
Only rust-worn tongues can pronounce
that the accounts of those who vacate their offices are all wrong,
and of those who take over, all clean and right.
Now the blacksmith who forges the sword believes,
it is he who inscribes victory.

Translated from Urdu by Yasmeen Hameed

We Sinful Women

We, here, are the sinful women,
undaunted by the grandeur
of the richly robed—
we neither sell our lives
nor lower our heads
nor fold our hands.

We, here, are the sinful women.
Those who trade in the harvest of our bodies
stand victorious,
courtiers of distinction,
arbiters of the wealthy.

We, here, are the sinful women—
when we set forth holding aloft the banner of truth,
we find roadways draped in falsehood,
on each threshold tales of damnation,
find tongues that could have spoken slit.

We, here, are the sinful women—
even if night comes in pursuit,
these eyes will not be blotted out,
for now that the wall has been torn,
do not insist on raising it again.

We, here, are the sinful women,
undaunted by the grandeur

of the richly robed—
we neither sell our lives
nor lower our heads
nor fold our hands.

Translated from Urdu by Yasmeen Hameed

SHABNAM SHAKEEL

Curse of Infertility

Lo, night once again writhes in labor,
an ancient hurt that is its fate since time immemorial.
Its face begins to darken
with pain and anguish.
Racing through arteries,
diffused through every vein,
is a fear as well.
She is caught in that life-and-death struggle
which is vital to the act of creation.
In but a little while
she will have given birth to
an uncertain day
smeared with suspicion—
and seeing it
will rise to her lips but one malediction:
Next time, Almighty God, may my embryo be still!

Translated from Urdu by Yasmeen Hameed

Elixir of Life

An ardor that expired in its prime,
an ideal, shattered,
a dream, unfulfilled—
you lament these,
carry within you a lingering heartache,
an anxiety keeps you continually restless.
In the city of memories you sit behind closed doors.
Recall the soothing hours that have passed,
that brought with them intimations of incompleteness,
and be grateful to your ruling stars
from whose orbits you received
wisdom to discern the ecstasies of anguish.

Whenever anyone here
attempted to hold time's sand in a fist,
or clip the wings
of a moment floating away like a butterfly
to preserve it for an eternity,
ardors crumbled in desperation,
the aspects of dreams lost their shape
and aspirations became baffling sphinxes,
as if they had not a grain
of desire to survive.
Perhaps the elixir of life does not suit them at all.

Translated from Urdu by Yasmeen Hameed

Every Dream of Ours, Framed by the Hereafter

Each day of mine, pledged to the day after
the present perpetually I hazard as wager
bind to the cross
mingle in dust
venerating each day after, squander the day that is
and sit bewailing
that what is obtainable today
may not be snatched away tomorrow.
What have I not done in this apprehension, this fear—
postponed every pleasure to the day after
for the day after considered it permissible to strangulate the present.
A murderer, but how can anyone recognize me
since in tomorrow's casket
wearing the victim's face I lie
but on my hands
these spots of blood
with whom should they plead
who invoke as judge?
Where, where, should they go?
If only there were someone
to listen to their pleas
offer them justice
find me guilty
and in the casket of tomorrow
drive the last nail.

Translated from Urdu by Yasmeen Hameed

Ghazal: I Am Schooled in Scriptures of Grief

I am schooled in scriptures of grief
I have grown up in wretchedness

They'll just be a waste of time
the things in which I am involved

Is this my empire and my throne
or am I on the gallows tree?

Half of me is above the sand
the other half is buried beneath

I have granted half of his request
I am holding out on the other half

It is not easy to knock me over
I am standing on my own two feet

Translated from Urdu by Waqas Khwaja

Heritage

I

Easy nights, easy days—
I am neither discontented in the day
nor have nights of sleeplessness.
My life passes in great peace and comfort
for there is no place in my lap for sparking passions.
The caravan of life journeys on a settled road,
contrary or corresponding, the breeze brings no relief.
Clouds may burst with rain, but no more is the window flung open,
even at the blooming of a rose the fetters do not stir.
Snipping flowers, I fix them in a vase
as if it were a duty that must be observed.
I have nothing to do with moonlit nights—
what is there to obtain from the conversations of stars?
A sky, crowded or empty, has no meaning,
I now have no interest in useless things.
I have the books, but I cannot read them,
they look nice arranged in a certain order.
Where are they, those old pictures I had?
There were some letters, too, which I burned long ago.

II

The world has taught me new rules and practices now:
"It is proof of ill-breeding to laugh loudly,"

"How noisy it gets when birds twitter!"
"It is never good to go beyond limits in love,"
"Compromise, even of one's principles, is accepted in this world."
Whatever the decision, I never take it too emotionally,
in this lies my good, perhaps, and in this my welfare.
I have erased now from my heart the name that was engraved there
hearing which this heart sometimes forgot a beat.
There is no place for such things in my world anymore.

III

This may all be good, but, I don't know why, still
I often think of something in my heart and become agitated
that now my look-alike, my fondly nurtured daughter,
is gathering the heritage of all my rejected, useless thinking
and is filling up her lap.

Translated from Urdu by Waqas Khwaja

IFTIKHAR ARIF

Dialogue

"Who is it behind the wind's curtain who plays with the candle's flame?
There must be someone.
Who confers the robe of lineage and plays with the flow of time?
There must be someone.
Who calls a veil the mystery of truth's light and plays with light beams?
There must be someone."

"There is no one—
no one anywhere.
These are illusions, fantasies of the deluded that seek the fealty of every
    questioner
and soon strangle the questioner from within."

"Then who is it that stamps the sun on the tablet of moving waters and
    tosses up clouds?
Who stretches the clouds across seas and molds a pearl in the womb of
    an oyster shell?
Who is the planter of possibility, of fire in stone, color in fire, light in color?
Who inhabits dust with sound, sound with word, and word with the
    provisions of life?
No, someone is there—
somewhere someone there is.
Someone there must be."

Translated from Urdu by Waqas Khwaja

It Will Take a Few More Days

It will take a few days
to forget the destruction of a city like the heart.
It will take a few more days
to forget all the chaff and straw
all the cypresses and firs of this colorful world.
On the shore of exhausted dreams
somewhere a small house of hope
was almost complete.
It will take a few more days to forget that house.
But just how many days are left?
One day, on the heart's waiting tablet
suddenly
night will descend
and fulfill every dream that hides
in the treasure house of my lightless eyes—
will turn me, too, into a dream
such a dream, the desolate lap of which
has no blessing, no bright day.
It will take a few more days.

Translated from Urdu by Waqas Khwaja

Orientation

On the shore of the Euphrates
or some other river's side
all hordes are the same
all daggers are the same.

Light trampled under horses' hooves
light spreading from the river to fields of slaughter
light terrified in burned-down field tents—
all sights are the same.

After each such scene a silence falls
this silence is the note of complaint, the dialect of protest.
This is not a recent story, it is an ancient tale
the complexion of endurance in each telling is the same.

On the shore of the Euphrates
or another river's side
all hordes are the same.

Translated from Urdu by Waqas Khwaja

The Last Man's Victory Song

The Shah's fellows are satisfied that desecrated heads and
    chopped-off arms
hang from the city's walls.
There is peace everywhere,
peace and silence.
The anguished cries sacrificed to the patrols,
the merchandise of patience offered up to the desolation of prayer,
the hope of recompense yielded to uncertainty of reward—
there is neither trust in the word nor respect for blood.
Peace and silence.
The Shah's fellows are satisfied that desecrated heads and
    chopped arms
hang from the city's ramparts and there is peace everywhere.
The river of power is planked with the bodies of rebels,
whatever spoils could be seized have been shared,
ropes of the canopy of speech and language have been cut—
it is such a state, even the desire for safety is madness.
Peace and silence.
The Shah's fellows are satisfied that desecrated heads and
    chopped-off arms
hang from the city's walls,
and there is peace everywhere.
Peace and silence.

Translated from Urdu by Waqas Khwaja

Twelfth Man

In pleasant weather
crowds of spectators
come to applaud
their teams,
everyone cheers their
favorite players.
Apart and alone, I
hoot
the twelfth man.
What a strange player
is the twelfth man!
The game goes on,
the din and clamor persist,
applause continues,
and he, apart from everyone,
awaits
such a time,
such a moment,
when some mishap occurs
and he comes out to play
in the midst of clapping.
A word of praise,
a cry of appreciation,
may be raised for him—
along with all the other players,
he too may gain stature.
But this seldom happens.

Even so, people say
that the player's relationship
to the game
is a lifelong affair.
This lifelong relationship
can also come to an end,
with the final whistle
the heart that sinks
can break as well.
You, too, Iftikhar Arif,
are the twelfth man,
waiting
for such a moment,
such a time,
when an accident happens,
when a mishap occurs.
You, too, Iftikhar Arif,
will sink,
you, too, will founder.

Translated from Urdu by Waqas Khwaja

AMJAD ISLAM AMJAD

Look, Like My Eyes!

You are at an age
when to pluck stars and bring them from the sky
seems truly possible.
Every flourishing part of the city
appears like your backyard,
it seems as if every day
every sight
seeks your permission to determine its shape—
what you wish, happens; what you think becomes possible.
But, heedless girl, you who wander entranced in the pouring
    rain of your unripe years
this cloud that today stops over your roof to speak to you
is an apparition.
In every season before and after you
on every rooftop, in the same manner
it goes about dispensing its deceptions.
From the morning of creation to the night of eternity, just one
    play and just one scene,
are rehearsed for the eye.
Sweet girl, who sleeps and wakes on the bed of dreams,
may your dreams live.
But keep in mind that all the sights of this dream-house of life
are prisoners of time, which, in its flow
carries them along and spurs them on.
The watching eyes are left behind.
Look . . . like . . . my eyes!

Translated from Urdu by Waqas Khwaja

Then Come, O Season of Mourning

Then come, O season of mourning—this time too, I again
take you by your finger and bring you home.
Everything there is still the same, nothing has changed.
Your room is just like it was, the way you
saw it, left it.

On the nightstand by your bed, even today
lies that coffee mug
on whose dry and broken rim
flecks of the froth of doubt and desire are still evident,
the pen, on whose nib the ink of sleepless night flakes
like the thin crust formed on dry lips.
There are those papers
which remain forever wet with some unwept tears.
Your sandals have been kept as well
to whose useless soles cling all those dreams
that, despite being so badly battered, still draw breath.
Your clothes
which came washed in sorrow's rains
still hang in my closets.
The damp towel of reassurances
and the half-dissolved soap of choking sobs
lie in the glistening washbasin.
To this day both the hot and cold faucets
continue to flow, which you that day
in some hurry left running.
The clock hanging on the wall beside the door

even now, as always
is slow by half a minute—
the date stuck on the calendar has not blinked an eye.
And suspended next to it
that one picture in which she
sits beside me with her head on my shoulder.
A butterfly close to my neck and her hair
flutters happily about.
Such a magic spell is cast
that it feels as if the heart is stopping, the breeze still blows.

But, O season of mourning
that very moment
who knows from which direction you came by
and passed between us—
passed between us in such a way
as a boundary separates opposing paths
on every side of which rises only the dust of separations.

A thin coat of that dust
perhaps you will see on the doorbell.
Perhaps some imperfection, too, you will notice in the picture.
The longing eyes that always used to smile,
you will, perhaps, now find the corners of those eyes a little wet.

Translated from Urdu by Waqas Khwaja

You Are in Love with Me

What is this childishness that nature has preserved
in love's disposition—
that however old, however strong it is,
it continues to need fresh affirmation?

You flourish in the heart to the furthest limit of certainty
distill from the eyes, glitter in the blood
and create a thousand endearing haloes of light.
But still you need the express words—
for love demands evidence of its existence
as a child who plants a seed in the evening
and rises again and again in the night
to see how much it has grown.

Love's disposition has this strange liking
for repetition
that it never tires of hearing words of reassurance.
In the time of parting or the moment of conjunction
it has but one passion—
say you love me,
say you love me.
You are in love with me.

Far deeper than oceans, brighter than stars
firm as mountains, enduring as the winds
all lovely sights from earth to sky
are tropes of love, are metaphors of devotion—
our own.

For us these moonlit nights adorn themselves
the golden day emerges—
wherever love proceeds, the world goes with it.

There is such unrest in the lands of love
it keeps lovers perpetually uneasy—
like scent in flower, like quicksilver on the palm
like the evening star
lovers' dawn resides in night.
In the small branches of doubt love's nest is built
harboring fears of parting even in the midst of union.

When pilgrims of love come to the end of their journey
picking up splinters of their exhaustion
wrapped in *ajraks* of their devotion
they pause at the last boundary of time.
Then someone, holding on
to the sinking thread of breath
softly says:
"This is truth, isn't it!
Our lives were allotted to each other.
This mist spread near and far from our eyes,
this is affection.
You were in love with me—
you were in love with me!"

In love's disposition
what is this childishness that nature has preserved?

Translated from Urdu by Waqas Khwaja

Poem for Those Affected by Disaster

They will publish the picture of your father's
disfigured face in the newspaper.
Hugging your daughters' torn garments,
they will listen to the account of your life-and-death
    sorrows
as if it was a folktale.
A lot of them will nod their heads in sympathy.
But who will share your grief?
Who will go out looking for you?

Children in ill-fated lanes
go about picking up pieces of dry bread—they will
    go on doing so.
Women in green fields
pick the crops—they will go on doing so,
continue weaving gowns and robes from new
    seasons.
But who will cover your naked body?
Who will go out looking for you?

For you, the rulers
will collect donations from country after country.
Tickets will be sold
for exhibits of posters of your dead body.
God-fearing citizens will buy gifts of prayers.
You will be publicly buried
amid gold-robed shouts.

But no one will die your death.
Tell me, who will go out?
Who will go out looking for you?

Translated from Urdu by Waqas Khwaja

Strange Desires

I have strange desires
Sometimes the desire to tuck the moon into my pocket
and wander about in dark lanes
Sometimes, in the blast of heavy rains
the desire to hold your body
Sometimes, while walking,
suddenly the desire for separation
Sometimes the wish to stay up all night
sometimes to sleep late into the morning
sometimes secretly to watch
girls bathing
or to go back to college in old age
Sometimes a burning desire to renounce the world
sometimes the desire to battle the whole world
Strange desires
One day I will be terror-stricken by the mysterious shadows
    of these desires
You will see, one day, just like this I will die

Translated from Urdu by Waqas Khwaja

FAHMIDA RIAZ

Aqleema

Aqleema,
born of the mother
of Abel and Cain,
born of the same mother
but different,
between her thighs,
in the fullness of her breasts,
and inside her belly,
and in her womb.
Why is the fate of them all the sacrifice of a fatted calf?
She, the prisoner of her own body,
in the fierce sun
stands atop a burning rock.
Look carefully at the imprint in the stone.
Above the slender thighs,
the intricate womb,
Aqleema has a head, too.
Allah, speak sometimes to Aqleema too,
ask something!

Translated from Urdu by Yasmeen Hameed

The Chador and the Walled Homestead

My Lord, what shall I do with this black chador?
Why do you (many thanks, though) bestow it upon me?
I am not in mourning that I should wear it
to show my sorrow and grief to the world,
nor am I stricken with disease that I should drown myself in the
    darkness of its folds,
not a sinner or a felon
that I should be forced to mark my forehead with its black ink—
not meaning to be impudent, my Lord.

If my life be spared,
I would with folded hands point out,
O noble master,
that in your perfumed chamber lies a corpse,
decomposing—who knows, how long it has lain there—
that needs your compassion.
Sir, show it a little kindness.
Don't give this black chador to me—
cover the shroudless corpse in your chamber with this black sheet,
for the stench that rises from it
pants down every street,
strikes its head against thresholds and doors,
tries to cover its nakedness.

Listen, its heartrending screams
conjure strange illusions.
They, who are naked even in their chadors—

who are they? You must know.
My Lord, surely you recognize them?
These are concubines!
Hostages, who remain lawful for the night,
and at dawn are sent away.
These are bondswomen!
Raised in status by the planting of your Honor's holy seed.
These are the household ladies
who, to offer the tribute of their wifehood,
stand row after row awaiting their turn.
These are mere girls,
on whose head, when my Lord places his affectionate hand,
their virginal blood flows to bring color to his gray beard.

In my Lord's perfumed chamber, life has wept its course in blood—
where this body lies
the slow murderous centuries have flaunted this bloodcurdling spectacle.
Put an end to the show!
Cover it up, my Lord!
The black chador has come to be not my need but your own,
for on this earth my existence is not simply a sign of lust.
My intellect sparkles on the grand avenues of life,
the sweat on the earth's face gleams with my labor.
These walled homesteads, this chador, the rotting carcass—they can have
    these blessings.
In open air, with sails spread wide, my ship will ride the seas.
I am the traveling companion of the new Adam
who has won my trusting fellowship.

Translated from Urdu by Yasmeen Hameed

Search Warrant

Police Chief:
"Look, Bibi, I have a search warrant,
troopers too, waiting around the corner of this street.
I could do this on my own, I thought—
one item is all we need.
Why resist and risk dishonor? So hand it over on
    your own
or simply say where in the house you've hidden it."

Never had I seen my home this way before.
I hear heartbeats throb in its doors and walls,
from arteries of stone and steel seeps blood,
warm breaths, eyes wide open, parted lips on all sides,
whispering softly in my ear, repeating one more time
my seven-generations' pledge to my country's dust.
Four walls, O my homeland, in your lap,
A brief period of security, this is my debt to you.

How many underground prison cells rise before the eyes!
How many possibilities disclose their doors to me today!
At my feet opens the tunnel of my hopes
on whose walls glimmer the rainbow colors of life.
Now new themes will be inscribed on the city's
    surrounding walls,
O passing moment! I swear by your trampled honor.

Dust in the lane where my house stands is red,
beyond this window a red tulip blooms.
Such alarm on account of a book from the past?
Part this curtain and behold my dreams for the future.

Translated from Urdu by Yasmeen Hameed

NASREEN ANJUM BHATTI

Ascending Mystic Song

On the first step, Lord and Master, I stood amazed.
On the second step, Lord and Master, I caught sight of you.
On the third step, Lord and Master, God came close.
On the fourth step, Lord and Master, I found my love.
On the fifth step, Lord and Master, I rolled back the ages.
On the sixth step, Lord and Master, my heart was fearful.
On the seventh step, Lord and Master, I saw a dream.
On the eighth step, Lord and Master, I broke in two.
On the ninth step, Lord and Master, I was left all alone.
On the tenth step, Lord and Master, I cried out for you.
This pavilion of my love was raised in your name.
Without you, the noise and chatter is altogether worthless.

Translated from Punjabi by Muhammad Shahid and Waqas Khwaja

I

I lit a lamp and placed it in a shrine
keeping watch.
I am like water in a pitcher—
if you retain me, I remain.
He went by, himself, thoughtless,
whose thoughts engulfed me.

Translated from Punjabi by Muhammad Shahid and Waqas Khwaja

It Could be Any Age

Quietly, within, they tear at the roots of my being—
your eyes, Ranjhan.
Eyes, O my world!
The trident of a fleeting glance—
the body kindles, transforms.
Delights of love, different in daytime and at night.
We are guests of the rising moon,
Sacrificing sleep to its lamplight, our wakefulness imprisoned.
Summon our night!
The wedding party is ready to depart.
Farewell! Farewell! everyone calls out, the drum is struck.
At what hour would someone wink and say,
The night is over?
A moment's pause, a breath or two—
but no!
When does the night that has passed ever return?
What is written in fate cannot be altered: it will surely be.
The feet that slip put forth no roots, spring stretches and turns,
the body kindles, transforms.
Declining, old and seasoned now, caught in the beloved's bonds,
life completes itself this day.
I will become water and live in your eyes.
It could be any age.

Translated from Punjabi by Muhammad Shahid and Waqas Khwaja

Kafi

An ancient land, shaken with violence, pulled apart thread by thread,
a roll of ginned cotton, a bunch of cotton locks, a boll in a damp husk,
then bud, then seed—
in the end dust returns to dust to erase all difference.
Turning around, we return to our beginning.
However One commands!
I lit the shrine's lamp to earn love,
the lamp lit, night sped, but day did not dawn.
She who grinds is left to wait—
Who would toil so hard, O lighted lamp, if one is still to remain unfulfilled?
I, too, am but clay, I crack and shatter, there's nothing within, ah!
Needlessly I laid a wager—
there is no oil, no smoke, no kindling,
neither lamp wick nor wad of cotton dipped in oil.
Centuries are sewn around their origin,
the past drifts only farther.
With heavy heart, a crane takes to the air,
to join the flock it was parted from in flight—
they wheel and turn again and again,
searching in vain.
What luck, Ranjhan, you chanced my way!
I abandoned all caution, all sense of shame.
Why I bound my heart to Ranjhan, I have never understood.
Fiercely the firewood burns; crowds converge to warm themselves.
I long for Ranjhan, and a multitude gathers to stare at me.

Translated from Punjabi by Muhammad Shahid and Waqas Khwaja

The Sparrows' Question

Whom should we ask, dear blue-skinned love?
Is it morning, or has sleep fled in the middle of night?
Drums thunder and throb,
the sparrows are startled,
nestlings chirp for food.
Drums beat, and the sparrows fall stunned.
Beaters clop and clump through,
a struggle among trees—
leaves shake, the dust of blossoms falls, rulers are replaced.
We are but sparrows, blue love.

Seasons play their games.
We have seen people come and go,
seen the great and powerful—
but what does it matter to us?
We are but sparrows, blue love.

Once we take flight, we travel far,
tired and weary, settle upon a ledge.
Someone is awakened, another stares, one looks on in pity.
Someone listens for a moment
or angrily shouts a curse,
claps sharply once and never looks our way again.
It is the Lord's wish.
A lifetime of hardships has taught the sparrows how to suffer,
into deepest darkness the sparrows have descended.

Translated from Punjabi by Muhammad Shahid and Waqas Khwaja

YASMEEN HAMEED

Another Day Has Passed

The breath's smoke clings to all the windows,
again a city disappears.
In the playhouse of day and night, only I remain
and this fortress of stone and brick.
There are footfalls of bleeding apprehensions.
Creeping lizardlike
a crowd of loquacious women rustles
toward me.
The branch flowering on the heart's window wilts with the heat of pain,
someone's disapproving glance stops at the frontiers of trust.
And today, too, it transpired that
the special condition of love's contract
was consigned to the account of a paper relationship.
Every page of the heart's book is witness
that the book has remained unread.
When the scratch of the black reed-pen cried out
the careworn circle of hearing contracted—
someone's name separated from another's
and expectation drew a line across the country of hearts.
When winds spoke
all the inhabitants of the house switched off the lights and went to sleep.
Another day has passed.

Translated from Urdu by Waqas Khwaja

I Am Still Awake

I am still awake
like my eyes
and speak
in my own voice
my own dialect.
I have only now become acquainted with the meaning of migration.
When, sometimes, snow knocks a hole in the wall of night
I fill the hole with my body
and speak of the coming day.
All things placed in my room are awake—
they all address me
saying
death has some connection to flowers.
The smell of flowers in the vase
is the smell of flowers scattered on a fresh grave.
Springing from earth,
displayed in stores, do flowers know
they have some connection to death?
Flowers, too, are not enough—
for life or death
they don't fill up all the wounds
and start to wilt so soon.
But I remain awake, like my tears
and remember those things
I used to like
before the flowers spoiled.

Translated from Urdu by Waqas Khwaja

I Have Spat Out This Poem

I have spat out this poem
There, lick it up
with your long tongue
I endured
and changed your name
I swallowed fire
and did not consider you the sea
I took pride in my earth-brown complexion
and pride in the color of your blood
and laughed at the color of your blood
I drank up my teardrop
and dried up like the desert
I spent the night
and did not wait for morning
shattered the lamps
and burnt my hands
flung their ashes
to the seventh sky
from which no one wishes to return
Picking pearls from seashells
I tossed them into the sea
and filled my fists with glass
Have you ever seen the color of actual blood?
No, this is not a wound
I have covered the wound
and filled the cut with my own flesh
given away my eyes

and pieces of my body
made another human
If I were God
I would have blown my breath into it!

Translated from Urdu by Waqas Khwaja

In Our Station

Some people are born sad
and kept sad
so that they may make the world beautiful
We fell in love with grief
and the human being ceased to matter
Sunflower seeds slipped
out of our fists and broke into bloom
and doves' eggs were preserved
We drew a picture of a water tank
and changed the color of water
When pieces of paper fell from our hands
pens, small and large, broke into speech between our fingers
sarangi strings melted on our fingertips
and we taught peacocks how to dance
When we were advised to distill perfume from filth
we decided to move away
and disappeared in the crowd
With the last gleam of night
we found the poem's title
and in the company of those in deep sleep
were appointed to awaken others
In our station
there was no date for relinquishing our charge
That is why we should not be asked any questions
about the beauty or ugliness of the world

Translated from Urdu by Waqas Khwaja

The city glitters
and in some dim light you, too, are sleeping.
From these heights
the moon's surface is closer.
But, no—
no one knows
whether the air is swift or cold here,
whether this is a floating smoke of clouds
or the dust of companionship.
Is this the quivering wave of the final call
or the unsteady vessel of flight
or the lurching earth below?

Who was it went to sleep holding sand in his fists
became distant even to imagination and dream
disappeared in the tangled hair of straying night?
Are the stars moving with me?
What regret is it that has not yet been soothed?
Heights, separations
even intimations of death have not eased it.
Fellow traveler of depths
of altitudes
tell me—
on earth
in the air
the path that never took shape
what came of it?

Tell me
what kind of sleep is it
that can cross the wall of night
and transform into morning?—

What kind of dream?
Tell me, what is this cry of pain in the air?
What is this restlessness?
The journey is coming to an end
and the noise is deafening.

Translated from Urdu by Waqas Khwaja

Who Will Write the Epitaph?

You are looking, just now, for the first star
but its light has not yet reached the eyes.
When, beyond the destination of defeat and dispersal,
hundreds of light-years have been subdued,
then you, at the utmost margin of the sky,
will be listening to stories about the earth-born.
From space within space
planetary systems will call to their sparsely inhabited
    worlds.
Earth, too, will start at the familiar knocking.
But, then, who will speak?
The rose garden, color, fragrance
twittering trees and roaring forests—
all alone, what will they do?
Day, night, wandering from town to town,
Day, night, wandering from town to town.
Whom will they pat to sleep, whom will they awake?
Warming themselves at a fire in some dismal village
to whom will the idle lines of hands
complain of their existence?
Who will commiserate
with the life of stones returning to ice?
When all the dreams of crowded galaxies in space
    within space,
dreams laughing at tales of love and parting,
after concluding their last rotation,

remain unexplained,
who will weep at this failure?
Who will write the epitaph of the earth-born?

Translated from Urdu by Waqas Khwaja

SEHAR IMDAD

Acid

To the nameless martyrs of Sindh

Needles stabbed in eyes,
some pleasant dream
turns to stone.

The jugular severed in the slit throat,
some melodious song
remains trapped in the heart.

Acid poured
over hennaed hands,
slowly skin crinkles and dies.

The sun's hot rays
prick like daggers.
Night, like poison,
runs through veins.

Translated from Sindhi by Azmat Ansari and Waqas Khwaja

Mohenjo Daro

(The Mound of the Dead)

From the land's
seven layers emerged
signs of a ruined settlement.
In the room of what was once a house
a human frame without flesh.
And I wonder,
my heart troubled,
whose skeleton is this?
Is it my own?

Five thousand years ago,
what would I have looked like?
And my beloved?
What sort of eyes did this skeleton have,
what was its face, its appearance—
were they like mine?
Like someone else's?
How did they look? How?

There must have been a heart in this frame—
that heart would have throbbed and quavered too.
And in those heartbeats must have lived she,
or he.

Translated from Sindhi by Azmat Ansari and Waqas Khwaja

Sun, Moon, Star

The *jaltarang* player and ecstasy!
Like a faraway brook
your laughter echoes,
the gleam in your eyes shimmers in the skies.

Moon and star, the sun and planets spin
in tune with you,
and with your melody the winds change course.
Your anger is the flash of lightning,
your cheerfulness inhabits the garden,
earth and sky are washed clean by your tears.
All creation is enamored of your signs and mysteries—
your playful glances cast a spell upon the world,
and the limitless ocean of time dances ceaselessly.

Translated from Sindhi by Azmat Ansari and Waqas Khwaja

Living but Dead

To whom do these shreds of flesh belong?
Whose are these?
No one knows.
This was a human body.
These remains were once part of a single body.

This is a foot.
This is a wrist.
This is a broken hand clutching at something,
and this is the head—
brown hair
in which a black ribbon a mother tied with her own hands
now dangles in the searing air
smelling of gunpowder.

These feet no longer run after butterflies,
the wrists no longer move.
The head that once lay on a mother's breast
is no longer attached to a body.
This is me, and this her third world.

Human beings are helpless, their hands tied,
their lips taped shut,
their necks bent toward the ground,
as if, living, they were dead.

Translated from Sindhi by Azmat Ansari and Waqas Khwaja

Tsunami

A few days ago
I had a name,
I had a mother,
I had a father.
Probably, there were a sister
and a brother, too.
What shared affections,
what priceless relationships!

A few days ago
laughter rang
in the courtyard of my home.
The black bee hung over the flowers,
the swing was crowded.

A few days ago
my mother's soft voice melted like honey in my ears.
In my eyes, how many of my father's dreams found a home?
Tender were the words spoken in this household.

A few days ago
I flourished in the shade of my mother's love,
holding on to my father's finger, I learned to walk,
and countless pet names were invented to indulge me.
Now, after the tsunami, I am only "Child #81."
The tsunami has robbed me of my name.

Translated from Sindhi by Azmat Ansari and Waqas Khwaja

PARVEEN SHAKIR

Ghazal: From Lane to Lane Spread the Rumor of Familiarity

From lane to lane spread the rumor of familiarity—
he greeted me like fragrance in the air.

How can I say he has abandoned me?
It is true, but it is a matter of embarrassment.

Wherever he went, returning, he came to me:
this is the only good thing in my inconstant lover.

Your embrace, like your heart, may be forever inhabited,
you may never face the desolation of a lonely night.

When he placed his hand on my burning forehead,
the effect of healing spread to the very soul.

Even now, in monsoon nights, my body hurts
and wondrous desires to stretch and yawn awaken within it.

Translated from Urdu by Waqas Khwaja

Ghazal: No Spirit Left to Proceed, Impossible to Stop

No spirit left to proceed, impossible to stop,
love's journey has utterly drained me.

O my land of roses, you wished for a book.
Look, though, what people of the Book have done to you.

When hearts drew close, we had a very different understanding—
At the time of parting, though, he raised a new issue entirely!

I could not put name and face together today,
what picture has time turned into dream and imagination?

Among various options, separation was mentioned too—
I made just a passing remark; what he did is beyond belief!

After all these years he remonstrated with me today.
Has he restored me, then, to the beloved's station?

Translated from Urdu by Waqas Khwaja

Misfit

Sometimes I wonder
why do I so much lack the art
of pleasing people?
Some are annoyed with my words,
others with my tone and tenor.
First, my mother
was unhappy with my busy schedule;
now my son
has the same complaint
(in the blind race to earn a living, how far back must
    relationships be pushed!)
when the reality is
that my household
enjoys the full benefits
of my obligation to play the part of a woman.
Every morning on my shoulders,
though, the weight of responsibilities
grows greater than ever—
still, every day
the reproach of incompetence on my back
becomes ever more insistent.
Then there is my workplace,
where the first condition of appointment is
to tender the resignation of all self-respect.
I try to grow flowers in barren minds—
sometimes a little green shoot becomes visible,
otherwise, stones

are often annoyed with the rain.
My tribe
manages to find light in my words,
but I
know very well
whose
eyes are on the word
and whose on the word's creator.
All circles are smaller than my feet,
but time's wild dance
stops nowhere.
The rhythm of the dance grows faster, faster—
either I am something else
or this is not my planet.

Translated from Urdu by Yasmeen Hameed

Soliloquy

It seems
that those around me
speak a very different language.
That wavelength
at which we had maintained communication
has shifted to some other range.
Either my lexicon has grown obsolete
or their idiom has changed.
The path on which my words take me,
for the meaning of that path,
they have a separate glossary.
I remain silent to preserve the sanctity of words,
and the only conversation
possible for me is with walls, with my loneliness, or my shadow.
I dread that moment
when, shriveling within myself,
I may forget even the frequency
that allows me to talk to myself
(keeps me in touch)
so that one day
I am left shouting only, "May Day, May Day!"

Translated from Urdu by Yasmeen Hameed

PUSHPA VALLABH

Singer

Dark night, a cluster of twinkling stars,
cold wind, the rustle of leaves,
and silence, from which the sounds of a *sarangi* emerge.
Shedding tears, the singer performs
to the accompaniment of the harmonium.

Her voice, rising from the heart,
and the harmonium's reverberating notes
become one—
there is no line of division
where voice
breaks free of the instrument
or tries to find its own way.
What is this raga that has no apparent form?
It flows with the blood,
and throbs in every vein and artery of the heart,
becomes a falling tear soaked up by the singer's *chunni*.
A star shoots across the sky.
Whose voice is this
that brings to mind the desert dunes?
The desolate sound of the instruments
draws tears down the singer's face.
In the pursuit of excellence the singer expires—
one person pays off the debt of melody for everyone.
Her sacrifice enriches the listeners
but leaves her destitute.

Translated from Sindhi by Azmat Ansari and Waqas Khwaja

I Am Without Form or Shape

I am water—
don't confine me in a jar,
don't force me to remain still.
I exist to flow forth,
to take my own course.

I am love—
don't assign me a color.
Whatever color I am painted,
that is my color.
Don't look for me in his eyes or her eyes.
I am in everyone's eyes.

I am prayer—
don't give me a form.
Whatever mold I flow into
I take its shape.
Don't search for my shape:
I have no shape.

I am the Torah, I am the Gospel,
I am Gita, I am Ramayana.
Don't look for me in books.
I am the invisible sign between words.

Translated from Sindhi by Azmat Ansari and Waqas Khwaja

Light a Lamp and See

So what if the tongue is silenced?
Let your fingers speak, and you will see,
feelings will repair
the broken words.

I cannot fly,
I know.
A fall would shatter me to pieces.
But wings will grow.
Spread your arms like a rope walker,
walk the rope and see.

Dreams tower and soar.
They cannot be fulfilled in this life.
Stars will climb down from the heights,
the sun incline toward earth—
just once,
embrace the clouds and see.

Every loss conceals a victory,
your lap will bloom with flowers.
Lose everything in love and see.

All the world seeks a guide,
the caravan will continue to swell—
just once,
play that melody on the flute and see.

There is absolute darkness,
the eye cannot make out the hand's shape.
Light will catch at light and grow—
it may be small,
light a lamp, and see.

Translated from Sindhi by Azmat Ansari and Waqas Khwaja

People Are the Same

Religion is my very soul.
Caught in words,
in the difference between words,
people have become estranged.
Some fight and wrangle,
some have developed a taste for blood—
they have not understood,
people of all religions are the same.
Beneath all colors, hearts are the same,
in everyone, the same emotions,
the same kind of thoughts.
Wound them, and the color of their blood is the same,
in grief, the color of their tears is the same.
In every heart,
the same Allah,
the same Ram,
the same Issa.

Translated from Sindhi by Azmat Ansari and Waqas Khwaja

A Small Desire

A small desire dwells
in my small heart,
like lamplight
in a darkened room.

The desire to soar in the skies,
to skim mountaintops—
the longing for such a life
that death cannot vanquish,
in my small heart.

To scud like clouds,
to fly like birds,
the wish to weave a band of stars
and wear them on my feet,
in my small heart.

The desire to be one
whom waters cannot sweep away,
nor fire burn.
The wish to be already past the sacred flame,
to be one whom the sword cannot injure,
the bullet cannot wound,
whom death cannot kill—
I desire such a life,
in my small heart.

Translated from Sindhi by Azmat Ansari and Waqas Khwaja

?

You can sit
looking at me, face to face,
talking to me in words that fascinate.
How enthralled you seem by my ideas and my art—
how enthralled by my lovely poems!
But a wrinkle in this fine gentleman's life
cannot be denied.
Sometimes,
for no reason, I too
call up that handsome man.
After I say "Hello" and a word or two,
he asks in a strange voice,
"Who is this I'm talking to?"

Translated from Pashto by Sher Zaman Taizi

Beautiful Book

How many questions did I have to ask
to discover the secret of your heart?
First,
Who else is in your life?
You said,
There's only this one book.
I persisted,
Your relations, at home, I mean?
You said again,
Just this book.
Right! But what's in your heart?
You were confused by that, somewhat—
God knows why.
Then, with great tenderness,
you took my face in your hands
and in a gentle, though slightly gruff, voice said,
This beautiful book!

Translated from Pashto by Sher Zaman Taizi

Life and Time

We grow up
but do not comprehend life.
We think life is just the passing of time.
The fact is,
life is one thing,
and time something else.

Translated from Pashto by Sher Zaman Taizi

Truth

Distance, too, is good.
Because you are far away,
I feel you are very close to me.
Yes—
but what of proximity, of union?
When you come near, then, my love, you are far away.

Translated from Pashto by Sher Zaman Taizi

Where, in the Ground Plan of Your Life, Do I Stand, My Love?

Far from the edifice that is your body,
I am far,
not just from your memory,
I am absent from the very kernel of your thoughts.
Deprived of the luxury of your body,
I no longer even exist in the islands of your words.
Even so, I make a claim on the house that is your heart?
How is it possible! It's a lie, dear.
With all these signs, tell me,
in the ground plan of your life, my love,
where is my place?

Translated from Pashto by Sher Zaman Taizi

Preface

p. xvi   *nazm and ghazal*
See Introduction for a brief explanation of these verse forms.

The Great Mosque of Córdoba

p. 5   *Jibraeel*
Gabriel.

p. 5   *Mustafa*
Literally, "The Chosen"—title used for Muhammad, the Prophet of Islam.

p. 6   *the being of light*
The reference is to angels.

p. 8   *La ila*
Literally, "No deity." The first two words of the primary Muslim declaration of faith, known as the first *kalma* or *Kalma-e-Tayyaba*, "declaration of purity." The full declaration is as follows: *La ila ha il Allah, Muhammad ur Rasul Allah*, "There is no deity or god but God (Allah), and Muhammad is Allah's Messenger."

p. 9   *Mecca of the Accomplished*
Iqbal here addresses the mosque directly.

p. 12   *Guadalquivir*
Literally, "great river" in Arabic.

Address

p. 15   *Mir Jafar*

The traitor who betrayed Siraj-ud-Daula, the governor of Bengal, in his final battle against the British at Plassey in 1757.

p. 15   *begums of Avadh*

The begums (ladies) of Avadh refers to the mother of Nawab Shuja-ud-Daula, ruler of Avadh, and his widow who were physically assaulted and robbed of their inherited assets by the British after the death of the Nawab in 1775. The "spoliation of the Begums of Oude" was one of the charges brought up in the impeachment proceedings for "high crimes and misdemeanors," initiated by Edmund Burke, Charles Fox, and R.S. Sheridan in the House of Commons in 1787, against Warren Hastings, the first Governor General of India. The House of Commons later acquitted Warren Hastings of all the charges.

p. 15   *Rani of Jhansi*

The Rani of Jhansi, Lakshmibai (1828–1858), neé Manikarnika, was the wife of Gangadhar Rao, Raja of the Maratha kingdom of Jhansi who died without a natural heir in 1853, opening up an opportunity for the British to annex the state on the basis of the East India Company's Doctrine of Lapse. The Rani of Jhansi resisted their maneuvers and led her army, comprised of both male and female units, against the British in the 1857 war, variously known as the Indian Mutiny, the Sepoy Rebellion, and the Indian Uprising Against Imperial Rule, among other designations. She was greatly admired for her courage, even by her enemies, and has become one of the iconic figures of India's struggle against British imperialism. She died fighting in the battle of Gwalior in 1858.

p. 15   *Bahadur Shah*

Bahadur Shah Zafar (1775–1862), the last Mughal Emperor, was almost eighty years old at the time of the so-called 1857 Mutiny. The rebellion against British rule was carried out by diverse groups of Hindus and Muslims in his name, although he neither endorsed the rebellion nor could take part in any of the battles.

After the fall of Delhi in 1858, the British sacked the city and exiled the old king with his wife to Rangoon in Burma, where he died in poverty a few years later.

p. 15   *Tipu*
Sultan of Mysore (1782–1799). Tipu (or Tipoo) Sultan, also known as "The Tiger of Mysore," was defeated by the British under Arthur Wellesley at the famous Battle of Seringapatam (1799), where he died fighting valiantly, though many of his commanders had been secretly bribed by the British. For many Indians, this marks the last stand against British expansion in India, and Tipu continues to be greatly revered as a patriotic and courageous ruler. Of course, the British portrayed him as a tyrant of the worst order.

p. 15   *Emperor Zafar*
While he was held prisoner by the British following the 1857 uprising, the Emperor Zafar was presented with the heads of his sons in a covered dish.

p. 15   *Mitya Burj*
Mitya Burj is the place in Kolkata (formerly Calcutta), where the new court of the exiled Nawab Wajid Ali Shah was located.

p. 16   *Qaisar Bagh*
Qaisar Bagh is the name of the palace complex, with gardens, mosque, and ladies' apartments, that Nawab Wajid Ali Shah constructed in Lucknow.

p. 16   *Ah, Akhtar!*
Refers to Nawab Wajid Ali Shah, last ruler of Avadh, who used "Akhtar" (literally, "star") as his poetic *Takhalus*, or pen name. He was forced into exile in Kolkata after Avadh was annexed by the British.

p. 16   *Jallianwala Bagh massacre*
Jallianwala Bagh, in Amritsar, was the site of the slaughter of hundreds of unarmed Indian men, women, and children, on the orders of Brigadier-General Reginald Dyer.

p. 16   *Bhagat Singh*

Bhagat Singh was a freedom fighter from the Punjab who was hanged as a traitor by the British.

p. 18   *Husain*

Husain was the nephew of the Prophet Muhammad. During the massacre at Karbala, he was a martyr to justice at the hands of Shimr, a general acting on the orders of Yazid (sometimes spelled "Yezid"), the second Caliph of the Umayyad Dynasty.

Come to Salvation

p. 25   *Pukhtun*

Or Pakhtun, Pashtun, Pushtun, or Pathan. A speaker of Pukhto or Pashto. But both "Pukhtun" and "Pukhto" are also used to refer to the code of Pukhtunwali—the Pukhtun way of life, which upholds fairness, justice, boldness, bravery, and honor. Pukhto also means Truth, and is used in that sense in the penultimate couplet.

p. 25   *Takbir*

The cry of "Allah u Akbar" ("God is great") is known as the Takbir.

p. 26   *Majnun*

A reference to the legendary lover Majnun (his actual name was Qays ibn al-Mulawwah) from the classical Arabian story *Layla-Majnun*. Majnun means "one mad with love."

p. 27   *Salman, Abuzar, or Bilal*

All three were companions of the Prophet Muhammad. Salman was a Persian, popularly known as Salman al-Farsi, who converted to Islam in Medina and was one of the scribes of the Qur'anic revelations. Abuzar, also known as Abu Dhar al-Gaffari (his real name was Jandab ibn Junadah ibn Sakan) was an early convert to Islam and a stout supporter of the Prophet's mission throughout his life. Bilal was an African slave who converted to Islam and was one of the dearest companions of the holy Prophet. He was celebrated for his *adhan* (or *azan*), the call for prayer.

p. 27 *kills his cousin*

In Pukhtun tradition, the first cousin, or *tarbur*, is considered an enemy, chiefly because of potential disputes over the inheritance of property.

Ghazal: None Has Such Bewitching Eyes

p. 29 *Marghalaray*
Literally, a pearl.

p. 29 *Kashmala*
Name of the girl addressed in the poem. Literally, "basil."

Ghazal: I Shall Always Go with the Brave Pukhtun

p. 34 *jirgas*
Pashtun council of elders.

p. 34 *tapa*
Village.

Death of Israfil

p. 40 *Israfil*
The angel who will blow the trumpet on the day of judgment. In Islamic tradition he is seen as a musician of exceptional sweetness who sings the praises of God in a thousand languages and is the inspiration for all melody and song in the heavens and on earth.

Hassan the Potter

An unpublished note on this poem by the author states that "Love is no doubt important to an artist; but his art and his means of livelihood are even more important. Even in its great intensity, love is meaningless in the end unless it turns into an élan vital for the artist and leads him to still greater creativity."

At the Sinai Valley

p. 57 *garden of Iram*
A fabled garden, built by King Shaddad in Aden, mentioned in the Qur'an.

He Knows Not What He Must Express

The poem satirizes Zulfikar Ali Bhutto, former Prime Minister of Pakistan, founder of the Pakistan People's Party, and his two ministers, Abdul Hafiz Peerzada and Maulana Kausar Niazi.

Partition

Daman read this poem at a mushaira with the Indian President Dr. Rajindar Prasad in the chair and Pandit Nehru, at whose invitation he was visiting India, in attendance.

Brother, Are You from Kunjah?

p. 67 *my brother*
In fact, he is her cousin. In Punjabi culture, it is normal to call one's cousin "brother."

p. 67 *mammi*
The wife of the mother's brother.

My Words Are Odd

p. 69   *Balnath's disciple*

In the widely popular Punjabi romance *Heer Ranjha* by Warras Shah (1722–1798), Balnath is the chief of the *Kanphatta* yogis (yogis with pierced ears), whom Ranjha approaches for *yog* or enlightenment after his beloved Heer has been married off against her wishes to Saida Khera.

p. 69   *Ranjha of fictional romances*

Ranjha is Heer's lover in the story of Heer and Ranjha, which occurs in many variations. The best known are the *Heer* by Damodar and *Heer Ranjha* by Warras Shah. In the Punjab particularly, and the Indo-Pakistan cultural tradition generally, Heer is seen as the soul and Ranjha as the body, and their love represents the yearning of each for the other.

Devadasi

p. 92   *Devadasi*

Literally "slave of the gods." Temple dancer. Among Hindus, devadasis were girls dedicated at the time of their birth (sometimes later) to the service of the gods by their parents, or else taken into such service because they had been abandoned or simply had no one to look after them. The poet provides the following note in which he somewhat romanticizes their position: "Devadasis are girls (most often attractive young virgins) who serve in Hindu temples, doing cleaning chores and performing dances of devotion to the stone statue of the idol. They are forbidden to marry, although they yearn for love. Hundreds of devotees come to the temple, where they kiss the idol, offer it fruits, and shower flowers upon it. Love rains on the idol, but it never spares a look for the poor virgin."

p. 92   *Layla, Shirin, Mansur*, etc.

Heroines of well-known folk romances.

p. 93   *saqi*

Cupbearer or server of wine, often a beautiful adolescent boy. Symbol of the beloved in Perso-Indian poetry.

O Ghani! O You Ass, Ghani!

p. 94 *Ghani*
The poet's name, but *ghani* also means "generous," "openhanded," "munificent."

p. 95 *Kausar*
Referenced in the Qur'an, this is a lake situated on the shores of heaven. Its water is said to be milky white and sweet as honey. Those who are able to cross the straight and narrow bridge, no more than a hair's breadth, into heaven will be able to drink from it, and its nectar will make them forget all their earthly unhappiness and sorrows.

Question or Answer

p. 96 *Mansur*
Mansur al-Hallaj, Persian Sufi, poet, and teacher, who lived from 858–922. He is known for his famous utterance "Innal Haq," "I am Truth," or "I am God," during one of his trances, and was imprisoned and later crucified on the charge of heresy for making this statement. He is widely admired in the Muslim world for his martyrdom in the cause of truth.

p. 96 *Yazid*
Second Caliph of the Umayyad Dynasty, who was responsible for the Massacre of Karbala in which Husain and a large part of his family, including women and children, were murdered. The event looms large in the imagination of Muslim poets and is repeatedly referenced in their works.

p. 96 *Bahlol*
A mad fakir who lived during the time of the Caliph Haroun al Rashid. He was known for making statements that seemed profound and foolish at the same time. Considered a saint, or a dervish, by many in the Muslim world.

Search

p. 98   *rabab*
A stringed instrument played with a bow.

Terminus

p. 104   *Chhanni Khachi*
The poem is set in a dreamscape—surreal, of course, but nonetheless containing precise, realistic details, and encompassing the past, future, and the present simultaneously. "Chhanni Khachi" is the invented name of a mountain located in this world.

p. 105   *jogan*
Hindu holy woman. A female yogi.

Dialogue

p. 112   *autaq*
A place where Sindhis host visitors. That someone has an *autaq* shows that he or she is a person of consequence.

Farewell to the Earth

p. 114   *thar*
Name of the desert that extends from Rajasthan in India to the eastern part of Sindh as well as the Punjab in Pakistan.

Spinning Party

p. 120   *Spinning Party*
Tarinjan, in the original Punjabi, is a longstanding tradition in the village culture of the Punjab: a gathering of young women, often unmarried, for spinning cotton, exchanging information, gossip, and socializing.

p. 120 *Heer, Ranjha*

The lovers in the well-known Punjabi romance *Heer Ranjha*. Kaido, Heer's maternal uncle, and the Khera family, her in-laws, are represented as villains in the story.

p. 121 *doli*

A litter or palanquin in which the bride is conveyed to her husband's home.

Koël

p. 129 *koël*

A singing blackbird. A member of the cuckoo family.

A Gecko's Mind

p. 139 *Abu Lahab*

Literally "Father of Fire," or "Father of Flame," so called because his cheeks were said to be flaming red. His real name was Abd-al-Uzza ibn Abdul Muttalib, and he was a paternal uncle of the Prophet Muhammad, though he bore his nephew a fierce and bitter lifelong animosity. A Qur'anic verse condemns him and his wife, an equally fierce opponent of Islam, to the everlasting doom of hellfire.

Political Advisor

This poem was written in response to a boastful claim by a famous poet that he had become an unofficial advisor to the military dictator Field Marshal Muhammad Ayub Khan, President of Pakistan from 1958–1969.

Siege

p. 165 *Qalandars*

Sometimes referred to as roving monks. Like "fakirs," qalandars are holy men or women who have renounced their spouses, friends, and possessions. They are meant to have no worldly assets whatsoever.

Ghazal: The Flower that Bloomed Beneath the Ground Is in My Heart

p. 170   *Bilquis*
The Queen of Sheba in Muslim tradition. She is highly regarded in Islamic tradition as a woman who recognized the true religion when she visited Solomon in his palace.

Ghazal: Who Gave the *Jhoomar* of Pale Leaves to Dust's Forehead?

p. 172   *jhoomar*
A bridal ornament worn on the forehead.

p. 172   *Kaf*
The abode of the *dev*s (giants), or gods, Kaf is a fabulous mountain range believed in certain Muslim folk traditions to surround the earth.

Kashmir Is a Lion

p. 174   *Pharons*
A *pharon* is a long, loose robe worn by Kashmiris.

Our Heritage

p. 175   *Zindabad*
"Prosper forever."

p. 176   *bismillah*
Literally, "In the name of Allah." Muslims say "bismillah" before commencing any good activity, work, or project. It may be repeated a hundred times during

the day, and is used here in its extended sense of being "a beginning," i.e., this is just the beginning of the struggle.

Romance of Imagination

p. 178   *sarangi*
A popular stringed instrument, played with a bow, in the Indo-Pakistan subcontinent, widely used as an accompaniment in classical singing performances. It is said to most closely resemble the range of the human voice.

The Road of Memory

p. 190   *Shah Murid, Jam Durrak, et al.*
Shah Murid (also "Sheh Mureed") was a fifteenth-century Baloch hero known for his skills in horsemanship and the martial arts. Jam Durrak was a mid-eighteenth-century Balochi poet, active at the court of Mir Muhammad Nasir Khan of Kalat. Mast Tawakli (also "Tawakali") was a nineteenth-century Balochi Sufi poet. Hani was the beloved of Shah Murid, and Sammo the love of Mast Tawakali. The reference to "Sangeen" is unclear.

p. 191   *dupattas*
Silk or muslin wraps or shawls of very light material that are thrown across the chest and shoulders or used for covering the head. Worn by women in Pakistan and India and seen to represent respect and honor for the wearer.

You Are in Love with Me

p. 222   *ajraks*
A colorful shawl from Sindh.

Aqleema

p. 226   *Aqleema*
Sister of Cain and Abel.

It Could be Any Age

p. 233   *Ranjhan*
An affectionate form of the name Ranjha.

Kafi

p. 234   *Kafi*
Classical form of Sufi poetry in Punjabi, Sindhi, and Seraiki.

Sun, Moon, Star

p. 247   *jaltarang*
A musical instrument comprising china or earthenware bowls filled with various quantities of water, producing different notes when struck with a pair of wooden sticks.

Singer

p. 255   *chunni*
Punjabi word for "dupatta." (See "The Road of Memory," above.)

AALI, JAMILUDDIN (1926–): Aali is a respected Urdu poet who has also written a number of popular national songs and who has revived the traditional genre of *doha*, known for its candid informality. His newspaper column, which focuses on intellectual and literary activities, is widely read, and has been collected into several books. He has also written travelogues, and having once worked in banking, has compiled a dictionary of economic terms. In 1991, Aali received the Pride of Performance award from the government of Pakistan, followed by the Hilal-i-Imtiaz (Crescent of Excellence) in 1998. The Pakistan Academy of Letters conferred the Kamal-i-Funn (Lifetime Achievement Award) on Aali in 2007. He lives in Karachi.

ABBASI, TANVEER (1934–1994): Abbasi was a medical doctor by profession. His first collection of poetry, written in Sindhi, was published in 1958. By the time of his death he had four further volumes of verse to his credit, as well as several collections of critical essays and translations.

AGHA, WAZIR (1922–): Born in Sargodha, Agha is a prolific poet, prose writer, critic, and literary editor. After completing a master's degree in economics, he received his PhD for a dissertation on the use of humor and satire in Urdu literature. In 1966, he launched the Urdu literary journal *Auraq*. Agha has published seventeen collections of Urdu poetry, five collections of essays, and sixteen books of criticism. He lives in Lahore. The government of Pakistan awarded the Sitara-i-Imtiaz (Star of Excellence) to Agha in 1995.

AMJAD, AMJAD ISLAM (1944–): Amjad is an Urdu poet and a distinguished playwright. He has published more than eighteen books and has twice been the recipient of the National Hijra Award for Urdu poetry. He has also received the Pakistani government's Pride of Performance (1987) and Sitara-i-Imtiaz (1998) awards. A selection of his poems has been translated into English under the title *Love Encompasses All.*

AMJAD, MAJEED (1914–1974): A native of Jhang, in what is today Pakistan's Punjab province, Amjad is regarded as one of the most important Urdu poets of the twentieth century. He wrote with a distinctive poetic voice, its range and depth unique in modern poetry, and commanded a variety of themes and innovative forms. Before joining the civil service, he edited a literary magazine, *Urooj,* but was removed from this post for writing a poem against the British Raj. A recluse, Amjad published only one collection of his verse during his lifetime. A second volume and his collected works were published many years after his death.

ARIF, IFTIKHAR (1943–): Arif was born in Lucknow and emigrated to Pakistan in 1965. One of the leading Urdu poets, he has published five collections of his verse to date. An English translation of a selection of his poems, *Written in the Season of Fear,* has also appeared. He has been a recipient of the Writers Guild Award (1984), the Faiz International Award (1988), the Naqoosh Award (1994), the Wasiqa-i-Aitraf, presented by the Hamdard Foundation (1994), and the Maulvi Abdul Haq Award (1995). The Pakistani government awarded him the Pride of Performance award in 1998, the Sitara-i-Imtiaz in 1999, and the Hilal-i-Imtiaz in 2005. He has served as the head of the Urdu Markaz, London; the National Language Authority and the National Book Foundation; and is former Chairman of the Pakistan Academy of Letters. He lives in Islamabad.

AYAZ, SHEIKH (1923–1998): Born in Shikarpur, in Sindh (today Pakistan's southernmost province), Sheikh Ayaz is regarded as the leading figure of twentieth-century Sindhi literature. His published work runs to more than seventy volumes, comprising poetry, short stories, memoirs, essays, aphorisms, and journalism. Well-versed in Urdu, he published two collections of his own work and a monumental verse translation of Shah Latif's *Risalo.* He practiced law and also served as the vice chancellor of Sindh University. For his work as a poet, he was awarded the Hilal-i-Imtiaz in 1995 by the government of Pakistan and also received the Writers Guild Award. A selection of his work is available in English as *The Storm's Call for Prayers*.

BANIHALI, TAOS (1933–2000): Banihali was born in the village of Banihal, in Kashmir. His published works include *Kashmir Ki Lok Kahanian* and *Rishi Nama*, as well as a versified Urdu translation of Sheikh-ul-Islam Nuruddin Rishi's letters, written originally in Kashmiri. Banihali's own verse is not known to have been published during his lifetime.

BHATTI, NASREEN ANJUM (1948–): Bhatti holds a master's degree in both Urdu and Punjabi. An imagist whose manner of poetic expression is intense and forceful, she is the author of two poetry collections, one in Punjabi and one in Urdu. Bhatti is the editor of *Apni Gawahi*, an anthology of autobiographical sketches of prominent women from the Indo-Pakistan subcontinent. She lives in Lahore.

DAMAN, USTAD (1911–1984): Born Chiragh Din in Lahore, Ustad Daman is the best-known Punjabi poet of the post-Partition Punjab oral tradition. He was a tailor by profession, and in the early days recited his revolutionary, anti-imperialist poetry at the nationalist political gatherings of the Indian National Congress, taking an active part in the freedom movement. At the time of Partition, his shop and house were burned down by rioting mobs and his wife and young daughter were killed. However, Daman decided to stay in Lahore and the newly created country of Pakistan. He remained, throughout his life, a fierce opponent of dictatorship, civilian or military, and all corruption and hypocrisy. His work was transcribed and published as *Daman dey Moti* after his death by devoted followers and admirers. The poems he wrote are still widely quoted in the Punjab as well as in other regions of Pakistan.

FAIZ, FAIZ AHMAD (1911–1984): Faiz was born in Sialkot, which now lies near the Pakistani border with Kashmir, and educated in Lahore. A committed socialist,

Faiz was one of the leading lights of the Progressive Writers' Movement. His leftist beliefs and his commitment to the cause of the poor earned him two prison sentences. The best-loved poet of his day, Faiz is generally regarded as one of the greatest lyricists of Urdu poetry. He began his career as a lecturer in English literature and later edited a major English-language daily, the *Pakistan Times*. Although his first volume of poetry, *Naqsh-i-Faryadi*, was published in 1941, he became widely known after the publication of *Dast-i-Saba,* poems written during his second term in prison, ten years later. After General Zia-ul-Haq's coup, Faiz went into exile in Beirut, where he edited *Lotus*, the journal of the Afro-Asian Writers' Association, until his return to Pakistan in 1982. Faiz was the first Asian poet to win the Lenin Peace Prize (1963). He died in Lahore. Faiz was posthumously awarded the Nishan-i-Imtiaz (Sign of Excellence) in 1990 by the government of Pakistan.

FARAZ, AHMAD (1931–2008): Faraz is one of the most important contemporary Urdu poets. Born Syed Ahmad Shah, he used Ahmad Faraz as his pen-name. He obtained master's degrees in both Persian and Urdu from Peshawar University, where he also worked as a lecturer for a number of years. Starting with his highly acclaimed *Tanha Tanha*, Faraz published thirteen collections of his poetry during his lifetime. His collected works, *Shahr-i-Sukhan Arasta Hai*, were issued in 2004. Faraz also wrote a number of plays in verse, some of which have been translated into English. He was awarded the Lifetime Achievement Award by the Pakistan Academy of Letters in 2000. He was also awarded the Hilal-i-Imtiaz in 2004, though he declined to accept.

GUL, HASINA (1966–): A well-known Pashto poet of the younger generation. Gul works as a broadcaster at Pakistan Broadcasting Corporation's Peshawar station. In addition to her collections of poetry—*Shpoon Shpole Shpelai, Khutah Khabray Kava*, and *Da Hum Hagasey Mausam Dey*—she is also the author of a monograph on the Pashto writer Afzal-Afzal Shauq. She lives in Nowshera, not far from Peshawar, in Pakistan's Khyber Pakhtunkhwa Province.

HAMEED, YASMEEN (1951–): Hameed is Writer in Residence at the Lahore University of Management Sciences, where she is responsible for developing and teaching courses in Urdu literature. An Urdu poet who writes with a distinctly modern sensibility, she has produced four collections of verse to date—collected in one volume in 2007 as *Doosri Zindagi*—and has received several prizes for her work, including the Allama Iqbal Award. Also an accomplished translator, Hameed has produced numerous English-language versions of Urdu poetry (including a number of the poems contained in the present volume), as well as both editing and translating an anthology entitled *Contemporary Verse from Pakistan*. Hameed has received the Fatima Jinnah Medal in 2006 as well as the Tamgha-i-Imtiaz (Medal of Excellence) in 2008.

IMDAD, SEHAR (1951–): A poet who writes in both Urdu and Sindhi, Imdad is the author of *Choddenh Chand Akaas*, a collection of her Sindhi verse. She is also a scholar, teaching at the University of Sindh, and has edited a number of Sindhi-language publications. Sehar Imdad was awarded the Tamgha-i-Imtiaz by the government of Pakistan in 2008. She lives in Hyderabad.

IQBAL, ALLAMA MUHAMMAD (1877–1938): Today revered as Pakistan's national poet, Iqbal was born in Sialkot, where he studied under the tutelage of his mentor, Sayyed Mir Hassan, at the Scotch Mission College. Impressed by Iqbal's keen intelligence and natural talent for both poetry and scholarship, Hassan encouraged his pupil to pursue his education further. After taking his master's degree in philosophy from the University of Punjab in Lahore, Iqbal went to Britain and was admitted to Trinity College, Cambridge, to study philosophy, while simultaneously studying law at London's Lincoln's Inn. Having qualified as a barrister in 1908, he was called to the bar in London, but he continued his studies, ultimately producing a dissertation on Persian metaphysics for which he was awarded a PhD by Heidelberg University. He emerged as a notable poet while he was still young and gained immense prestige and popularity in the literary circles of his day for his outstanding works of poetry, written in both Urdu and Persian. Collections of his poems have been translated into many of the world's major languages. Among his other works, *The Reconstruction of Religious Thought in Islam*, a collection of lectures originally given in English, is still widely used by religious scholars and reformists. While he was still pursuing his studies abroad, Iqbal developed an interest in politics, and, upon returning to India, he became an important leader of the independence movement. In 1930, in his presidential address before the annual meeting of the All-India Muslim League in Allahabad, he articulated his idea for the creation of a separate state for Indian Muslims. In 1947, this separate state emerged onto the world map as Pakistan. Now honored as *Mufakkir-i-Pakistan* (The Thinker of Pakistan), *Shair-i-Mashriq* (The Poet of the East), and *Hakeem-ul-Ummat* (The Sage of the Ummah—that is, the people of Islam), Iqbal never lived to see Pakistan become a reality: he died in Lahore in 1938.

IQBAL, ZAFAR (1932–): Zafar Iqbal is an Urdu poet known for his innovative approach to the *ghazal*. Two of his earlier collections, *Aabi-Rawan* and *Gulaftab* are considered landmarks in the development of the form in Urdu. He regularly contributes literary articles to newspapers. His complete verse was recently published in a three-volume edition titled *Ab Tak* (2004). He lives in Lahore and Okara.

JAFFERY, ADA (1924–): Jaffery, who was born in Badayun (now in north-central Uttar Pradesh, in India), is regarded as one of the great pioneers among modern Urdu poetry's female poets. She has published numerous collections, as well as an autobiography, *Jo Rahi So Bekhabari Rahi*; her complete poems are now available in a volume titled *Mausam Mausam*. Jaffery has received numerous awards, including the Adamjee (1967), the Tamgha-i-Imtiaz (1981), the Baba-i-Urdu (1994), the Wasiqa-i-Aitaraf (1994), the Quaid-i-Azam Adabi (1997), and the Pride of Performance (2002). In 2003, she was honored with the Kamal-i-Funn by the Pakistan Academy of Letters. She lives in Karachi.

JALANDHARI, HAFEEZ (1900–1982): Jalandhari was named for his birthplace, Jalandhar, which now lies in India's portion of the Punjab. Obliged to earn a living at an early age, he moved from job to job—keeping time for the railroad, selling perfume, and doing calligraphy—until he found his true calling, as a literary journalist, when he started the literary magazine *Ejaz*. In 1922, he settled in Lahore, the literary capital of the Punjab, where he worked at a number of monthly journals, as well as at the children's magazine *Naunehal*. He subsequently served as the editor of *Tehzeeb-i-Niswan* and of *Phool*, another magazine for children. In 1926, he joined the literary magazine *Makhzan* and in 1930 launched a literary weekly called *Karzar*. Among his collections of Urdu poetry are *Naghma Zar*, *Soz-o-Saz*, *Talkh aab-i-Shirin*, and *Chiragh-i-Seher*, as well as *Shahnama-i-Islam*, which is considered his magnum opus. Jalandhari also wrote poems and short stories for children and is the author of Pakistan's national anthem. He was given the name *Abul-Asr* ("Master of the Age") by his mentor, the Persian poet Maulana Ghulam Qadir Girami.

JALANDHARI, ZIA (1923–): Zia Jalandhari is the pen name of Sayyed Zia Nisar Ahmad, a native of Jalandhar. His first volume of Urdu poetry appeared in 1955, and three more followed; these were later gathered into a single volume entitled *Sar-i-Sham Se Pase-Harf Tak*, published in 1993. In addition, his complete works are available under the title *Kulliyat-i-Zia*, and English translations of his poetry have also appeared. The government of Pakistan awarded him the Pride of Performance in 2005. He retired from Pakistan Television in 1985, where he had served as managing director. He lives in Islamabad.

JALIB, HABIB (1928–1993): Born in Hoshiarpur, East Punjab, Jalib started writing poetry by the age of fifteen. He moved to Karachi after Independence, and in 1954 moved again to Lahore, where he lived until his death. Starting his career as a lyrical *ghazal* writer, Jalib soon became an influential political author. A poet of the people, Jalib dedicated his life to fighting tyranny and oppression, even when his work led to jail sentences and poverty. His books, which were mainly censored or banned outright during his lifetime, include *Barg-i-Awara*, *Sar-i-Maqtal*, *Ahd-i-Sitam*, *Harf-i-Murad*, *Goshe-mein Qafas Kay*, *Zikr Behtay Khoon ka*, *Iss Shehar-i-Kharabi Mein*, *Kuliyat-i-Jalib*, *Harf-i-sar-i-Dar*, and *Jalib Beeti*. The government of

Pakistan awarded him the Hilal-i-Imtiaz in 1993 and the Nishan-i-Imtiaz posthumously in 2008.

JATOI, JANBAZ (1924–1994): Jatoi wrote in Seraiki, producing poems that are generally regarded as unique in style and idiom, inspired by the folk traditions of the region. He is the author of the collections *Ardasan, Tanwaran, Hawaran,* and *Sassi.* In 1993, the government of Pakistan awarded him the Pride of Performance, and the following year he received the Khawaja Fareed Award, bestowed by the Pakistan Academy of Letters.

KAZMI, NASIR (1925–1972): Kazmi was born about 125 miles north of Delhi, in Ambala, but migrated to Lahore following Partition. A very popular poet of the *ghazal,* he was able to capture the experience of migration and the anguish of adjustment to life in a new country. In Lahore, he edited the literary magazines *Auraq Nau* and *Khayal,* as well as working at a local Radio Pakistan station. He produced several collections of Urdu poetry over his relatively short life, including *Barg-i-Nay, Dewan, Pehli Barish,* and *Nishat-i-Khawab,* as well as a verse play, *Sur Ki Chaya.*

KHAN, GHANI (1914–1996): A noted poet of the Pashto language, as well as a painter and sculptor, Ghani Khan was born in Utmanzai, in what is now the Khyber Pakhtunkhwa Province of Pakistan. He received a broad education, studying at the Jamia Millia Islamia in Delhi, and at Rabindranath Tagore's Shantiniketan in West Bengal, and subsequently in England and then the United States. His first collection of poems, *De Pinjray Chaghar,* was published in 1956, and a second volume, *Panoos,* in 1978. A combined collection of his works appeared in 1985. He is also the author of a short treatise on Pashto society, written in English. For his outstanding contribution to Pashto poetry and for his artistic work generally, Ghani Khan was awarded the Sitara-i-Imtiaz by the government of Pakistan in 1980.

KUNJAHI, SHARIF (1911–2006): Kunjahi was born in Gujrat, a town that today lies in the northeast of Pakistan's Punjab. A versatile man of letters, he earned two master's degrees, one in Urdu and another in Persian, and taught literature in a number of colleges. From 1981 to 1988, he was associated with the publications division of the Urdu National Language Authority. He then returned to Gujrat, where he spent the rest of his life, ultimately producing a total of thirty-three books. These included collections of poetry in Punjabi (*Jhatian, Audak Hondi Loo, Jagrate*), Urdu (*Sooraj Such Aur Sa'ai, Lamhon Ka Sehra*), and Persian (*Do Dil*), as well as Urdu translations of *Heer*, the famous Punjabi romance by the Sufi poet Warras Shah, as well as Bertrand Russell's *Road to Freedom*. Kunjahi also translated the Qur'an into Punjabi. His honors include the Nishan-i-Gujrat, presented by the Literary Award Council of Gujrat in 1980, the Tamgha-i-Imtiaz in 1983 and Pride of Performance in 2000, both awarded by the government of Pakistan, and then a symbolic crown bestowed by the Bazm-i-Ghanimat, a local literary organization established in the name of classical Persian Poet Ghanimat Kunjahi of Kunjah, Gujrat, in 2004.

MALIHABADI, JOSH (1894–1982): Born in the village of Malihabad, in the area around Lucknow, Josh Malihabadi studied at St. Peter's College in Agra, and passed his senior Cambridge examination in 1914. He went on to study Arabic and Persian and in 1918 spent six months at Rabindranath Tagore's Shantiniketan. His first collection of poetry appeared in 1921. He also founded and edited the magazine *Kaleem*, in which he openly wrote in favor of independence from the British Raj. In 1947, he became the editor of another magazine, the *Aaj-Kal*, Delhi. He migrated to Pakistan in 1955 and worked for the Anjuman-i-Taraqqi-i-Urdu, an organization promoting Urdu language and literature. Malihabadi was a prolific poet, known for his masterful command of the Urdu language and his strict observance of its grammar. He is popularly known as the *Shair-i-Inqilab* (Poet of Revolution). Although not all of his poetic work has been published, numerous collections have appeared in print, including *Shola-o-Shabnam, Junoon-o-Hikmat, Fikr-o-Nishat,* and *Mehrab-o-Mizrab.* He also wrote an autobiography entitled *Yadoon Ki Barat*, which is one of most read biographies written in Urdu.

MEERAJI (1912–1949): Meeraji was the pen name adopted by Muhammad Sanaullah Sami Dar, whose modern verse broke new ground in Urdu poetry. In his earlier years, he edited *Adabi Duniya*, Maulvi Salahuddin's literary magazine, and later worked for All-India Radio. He was also instrumental in establishing the Halqa-i-Arbab-i-Zauq, an institution that has played an important role in nurturing and encouraging new writers. Among his volumes of poetry are *Meeraji ke Geet*, *Meeraji ki Nazmein*, *Geet hi Geet*, *Paband Nazmein*, and *Teen Rang*. He died young, and a complete collection of his poems, titled *Kulliyat-i-Meeraji*, was compiled in 1988 by the Urdu Markaz, London, some four decades after his death.

NAHEED, KISHWAR (1940–): Educated in Lahore, Naheed is a prolific writer of both poetry and prose who has a keen interest in women's issues. Her numerous collections of modern Urdu verse and *ghazal* have been gathered into a volume titled *Dasht-i-Qais Main Laila*. She is also the author of numerous works in various genres of prose, as well as a translator and writer of children's books. She was presented with the Adamjee Award for Literature in 1969 and won the UNESCO Prize for Children's Literature in 1974. She has also been honored by the Pakistani government with its Sitara-i-Imtiaz in 2000. Naheed lives in Islamabad, where she heads a non-governmental organization for women artisans called Hawwa.

NASEER, GUL KHAN (1914–1983): Born in Nushki, in Balochistan, Naseer was educated in Quetta and Lahore. One of the founders of the Balochi nationalist movement, he went to prison a number of times for his political views as well as his revolutionary poetry. In 1972–73, he served briefly as a minister in the first elected government of Balochistan. Among his major poetical works are *Gulbang*, *Dastaan-i-Dosheen-o-Shireen*, *Shup Garook*, *Grund*, *Hon-a-gwank*, *Purang*, *GulGal*, and *Shablank*. Naseer has come to be regarded as the poet laureate of the Balochi people.

NIAZI, MUNIR (1928–2006): Niazi numbers among the most influential of contemporary Urdu poets. His short poems generate a subtle mystery by mingling elements of the real and the unreal. Numerous collections of his Urdu poetry have appeared, and the poems he wrote in Punjabi are also very popular. He received the Sitara-i-Imtiaz twice in 1995 and 2004 from the government of Pakistan and was honored with a Kamal-i-Funn by the Pakistan Academy of Letters in 2002.

NIGAH, ZEHRA (1935–): One of Urdu's best-loved female poets, Nigah rose to prominence in the 1950s, at a time when poetry was still predominantly a male domain. Her melodic renditions of her verse made her a popular figure at *mushairas*, where poets gather to read their work. Thus far, three collections of her poetry have appeared: *Shaam ka Pehla Tara*, *Waraq*, and *Firaq*. In recognition of her outstanding contribution to literature, the government of Pakistan awarded her the Pride of Performance in 2005. Born in Hyderabad, she now lives in Karachi.

QASMI, AHMAD NADEEM (1914–2006): Qasmi had a long and rich literary career, over the course of which he distinguished himself not only as a poet but as a short story writer, editor, and newspaper columnist, as well as being one of the leading lights of the Progressive Writers' Movement. In addition to his many collections of Urdu poetry, Qasmi produced sixteen volumes of short stories. From 1964 to the time of his death, he edited the literary magazine *Funoon*, in which the work of many new Urdu writers first appeared. He also served as the guest editor of the quarterly Urdu journal *Adbiyat*, published by the Pakistan Academy of Letters. He was awarded the Adamjee Award for Urdu Poetry in 1964, the Pride of Performance in 1968, the Sitara-i-Imtiaz in 1980, and in 1997 received a Kamal-i-Funn from the Pakistan Academy of Letters. The government of Pakistan awarded him the Nishan-i-Imtiaz in 1999.

RAHI, AHMAD (1923–2002): Born Amritsar, Rahi is the author of two collections of poems in Urdu, *Rut Aai Rut Jai* and *Rag-i-Jan*. He also produced a volume of poems in Punjabi, *Trinjin*, that critics hold in high regard. He is also well known for the stories, songs, and dialogue that he wrote for Punjabi films.

He has served as the convener of the Punjabi Adabi Sangat, the most prestigious literary forum of its time, and was awarded the Pride of Performance by the government of Pakistan in 1998.

RASHID, N. M. (1910–1975): Born in 1910 in Gujranwala, a town now in the northeast of Pakistan's Punjab province, Rashid was one of the pioneering figures of modern Urdu poetry. He worked for All-India Radio until he joined the United Nations, serving in numerous countries over his distinguished career. His first collection, *Marva*, published in 1940, was a revolutionary book of free verse, seen at the time as a radical break with tradition, until Rashid's subsequent collections—*Iran Mein Ajnabi, La=Insaan,* and *Guman Ka Mumkin*—made clear his deep connections to the history of Urdu poetry. He also translated a selection of modern Persian poetry into Urdu, and his complete poems are available as *Kulliyat-i-Rashid.*

RIAZ, FAHMIDA (1946–): Born in Meerut shortly before Pakistan came into existence, Riaz is regarded as one of Urdu's front-rank poets. She has given great thought to the issue of language and a working-class audience, often choosing a rustic diction for its familiarity rather than employing a more formal Persianized expression. Among her works are *Pathar Ki Zuban, Badan Durida, Dhoop,* and *Kiya Tum Poora Chand Na Daikho Gay?* Fahmida Riaz has also translated selected works of Rumi and Farogh Farrukhzad. Presently Fahmida Riaz is head of the Urdu Dictionary Board of Pakistan.

SAMANDAR, SAMANDAR KHAN (1901–1990): Samandar started writing poetry at an early age and soon became known for his longer poems. One such work, *Da Tauheed Tarang*—a verse interpretation of the holy *Kalma-e-Tayyaba*, the basic declaration of Muslim faith (*La ila ha il allah, Muhammad ur Rasul Allah*: There is no god but God, and Muhammad is Allah's Messenger)—is regarded as his most outstanding literary achievement. He wrote a number of other book-length poems (such as *Da Bilal Bang, Dayalam Soka,* and *Quran Jara*), as well a book on *ilm-ul-urooz*, the study of the rules of Urdu poetry, under the title *Joor Samandar.* His complete poems have been published as *Let Aular*. He also translated two of the poetry collections of Allama Muhammad Iqbal (*Asrar-i-Khudi* and *Ramooz-i-Bekhudi*) into Pashto. He was awarded the Tamgha-i-Imtiaz by the government of Pakistan in 1987.

SEHBAI, SARMAD (1945–): Sarmad Sehbai obtained his master's in English literature from the Punjab University, Lahore. He started his career as Program Producer with Pakistan Television Corporation and rose to become its Managing Director. His collections of Urdu poetry include *Un Kahi Batoon Ki Thakan* and *Neeli Kay So Rung*. He has also published a volume of Urdu plays titled *Kathputliyoon Ka Shehr*. He lives in Islamabad.

SHAD, ATA (1939–1997): Ata Shad became popular as both a Balochi and an Urdu poet at a young age. He was the author of two collections of verse in Urdu (*Sangaab* and *Barfaag*) and three in Balochi (*Rooch Gar Shap*, *Sahaar*, and *Nadeem*). He also compiled an Urdu-Balochi dictionary and the Balochi *Haft Zabani Lughat* (dictionary in seven languages). He received the Pride of Performance from the government of Pakistan in 1983, followed by the Sitara-i-Imtiaz in 1992.

SHAKEEL, SHABNAM (1942–): A poet noted for her elegant work in Urdu, Shakeel has published two volumes of poetry, *Iztirab* and *Shab Zad*, as well as a collection of short stories titled *Na Qafas Na Aashiana*. She is also the author of a book of sketches and critical essays, *Taqreeb Kuch To*. She has been active as a teacher, and her writing on women poets was published under the title *Khawateen Ki Shairi*. Shabnam received the Pride of Performance in 2004. She lives in Islamabad.

SHAKIR, PARVEEN (1952–1994): Born in Karachi, Shakir taught English for nine years before joining the Civil Service of Pakistan, and was a senior officer when she died in a road accident. Her romantic verse became popular early in her literary career. Her first collection of poetry, *Khushboo*, received the Adamjee Literary Award in 1978. Among her other collections are *Sad Burg*,

Khud Kalami, Inkar, Kaf-i-Aina, and her collected works, *Mah-i-Tamam*. She was honored with the Faiz Ahmad Faiz Literary Award in 1989 and with the Pride of Performance in 1990.

SHAMIM, AFTAB IQBAL (1933–): Shamim is an Urdu poet whose verse often gives voice to his social concerns and his protest against injustice. His collections of Urdu poetry include *Farda Nazad, Zaid Say Mukalama,* and *Gum Samandar*. He was awarded the Pride of Performance in 2005. He lives in Islamabad.

SHINWARI, AMIR HAMZA KHAN (1907–1994): Born in a village in the Khyber Agency (in what is now Pakistan's Khyber Pakhtunkhwa Province), Shinwari has been acclaimed as Pashto's *Baba-i-Ghazal* (Father of the Ghazal). A prolific poet, who wrote blank verse in addition to *ghazals,* he was also the author of numerous prose works, including a novel, and was the screenwriter for the first Pashto-language film, *Laila Majnu*. He became president of the Ulusi Adabi Jirga in 1951—an organization promoting Pashto culture—and the following year organized a literary society called Khyber-Pakhto Adabi Jirga, which likewise has played a very important role in promoting the Pashto language and literature. Regarded as a trendsetter in the area of Pashtu *ghazal,* he has also translated the *Kalam-i-Iqbal,* a selection from the Poems of Allama Iqbal, into Pashto. He was awarded the Pride of Performance in 1978, and the Sitara-i-Imtiaz was conferred on him posthumously in 1994 by the government of Pakistan.

VALLABH, PUSHPA (1963–): A poet who writes in Sindhi, Urdu, and English, Vallabh was trained as a doctor. She began her literary career during her student years, editing college magazines. Her poems have been published in a variety of well-respected literary magazines, including the Pakistan Academy of Letters' semiannual English-language publication, *Pakistani Literature*. She was presented with the Sindhi Adabi Sangat award in 1985, and a volume of her Sindhi poetry, *Dari-e-Khaan Bahi,* appeared in 1992. She lives in Karachi.

ZAIDI, MUSTAFA (1930–1970): Born in Allahabad, Zaidi migrated to Pakistan in 1951. In 1954, he joined the Civil Service of Pakistan, but his scandalous lifestyle resulted in his dismissal from government service. In 1970, he was found dead in his bed with his lover Shahnaz Gul beside him in a state of unconsciousness. It was determined after a court inquiry that both lovers had attempted to commit suicide by taking poison. As a poet, Zaidi produced a number of collections in Urdu, including *Mauj Meri Sadaf Sadaf, Shehr-i-Aarzoo, Zanjeerain, Koh-i-Nida,* and *Qaba-i-Saaz.* His collected works were published posthumously as *Kulliyat-e-Mustafa Zaidi.*

AZMAT AHMAD ANSARI is an explorer, researcher, producer of documentary films, actor, translator, journalist, and playwright. He teaches in an MBA program at the Institute of Business Administration in Karachi, offering courses in business administration, oral communication, advertising, and media management.

IFTIKHAR ARIF: see **Poets**

MEHR AFSHAN FAROOQI is an assistant professor in the University of Virginia's Department of Middle Eastern and South Asian Languages and Cultures. She specializes in the literary cultures of South Asia, especially the literary culture and history of north India, and teaches both Hindi and Urdu language and literature. Her most recent publication is the two-volume *Oxford India Anthology of Modern Urdu Literature* (2008). She is presently working on a monograph on the Urdu literary and cultural critic Muhammad Hasan Askari.

ASIF FARRUKHI was born in 1959 in Karachi and trained as a physician at Karachi University and then at Harvard. As a writer and editor, he has published several collections of short stories and literary essays and has translated widely from world literature into Urdu. He is also the founder and editor of the literary journal *Duniyazad*, which publishes literary works from Pakistani and other languages in Urdu translation. He lives in Karachi.

M.A.R. HABIB received his PhD from Oxford University. A professor of English at Rutgers University, he is the author of five books, including *An Anthology of Modern Urdu Poetry in English Translation* (MLA, 2003) and *A History of Literary Criticism: From Plato to the Present* (Blackwell, 2005).

YASMEEN HAMEED: see **Poets**

SALEEM KAMILI, a scientist at the Centers for Disease Control and Prevention in Atlanta, Georgia, and an associate editor of the *Journal of Clinical Virology*, is an ardent lover of Kashmiri and Urdu poetry. He came to the United States in 1996 on a research fellowship after completing his PhD in biochemistry.

PERVEZ KHAN, who writes under the name Pervez Sheikh, was born in Peshawar, where he is presently the principal of Government High School. He holds a master's degree in Urdu, Pashto, and English, and is the author of *Tauda Bakara*, a novel in Pashto. He also translates regularly from Pashto into English for the journal *Pakistani Literature* and other Pakistani publications.

KHURRAM N. KHURSHID has a PhD in English from the University of New Brunswick, Canada. His research areas include postcolonial literature, partition narratives, and Indian and Pakistani fiction. He grew up in Pakistan, where he taught English at various colleges of the Punjab University for a number of years.

OMER KHWAJA has an MA from the University of Chicago. His interests lie in social movement unionism. Having spent two years working as a professional organizer for community organizations and labor unions across the United States, he hopes to write the first ethnographic account in Urdu of the revival of organized labor in the U.S.

WAQAS KHWAJA, professor of English at Agnes Scott College in Atlanta, has a PhD from Emory University in Victorian fiction and teaches courses in nineteenth-century British literature, Romantic prose and poetry, postcolonial literature, and poetry writing. He has published three collections of poetry, *No One Waits for the Train* (2007), *Mariam's Lament* (1992), *Six Geese From a Tomb at Medum* (1987); a literary travelogue, *Writers and Landscapes*

(1991), about his experiences with the International Writing Program at the University of Iowa; and has edited three anthologies of Pakistani literature, *Cactus* (1986), *Mornings in the Wilderness* (1988), and *Pakistani Short Stories* (1992), which also contain his translations of works from Urdu and Punjabi. He was a practicing lawyer, newspaper columnist, and regular contributor to *The Frontier Post, The Pakistan Economic Review, The Pakistan Times, News International, The Nation,* and *The Friday Times* between 1985 and 1992 in Pakistan before relocating to the United States in 1994. He has also contributed scholarly articles to academic journals and publications.

GEETA PATEL, whose research has engaged the politics, poetics, and economics of violence, loss, and transgression, is an associate professor at the University of Virginia. Her book *Lyrical Movements, Historical Hauntings: Gender, Colonialism, and Desire in Miraji's Urdu Poetry* (Stanford, 2002) reads gender and sexuality in twentieth-century Urdu poetic movements that emerge out of the lyric of loss. She has translated prose and poetry from Sanskrit, Urdu, Hindi, Braj, and Awadhi.

SHAH MOHAMMED PIRZADA was born in a family of writers and poets in a village near Mohenjodaro, Sindh. Trained as a medical technologist at Karachi University, he is a well-known Sindhi poet who occasionally writes in Urdu and English. In collaboration with Asif Farrukhi, he has translated selected poems by Sheikh Ayaz into English, and has also published a collection of his own poetry.

Born in Ranchi, India, ALKA ROY is a writer, performance artist, and engineer who works with new technologies in Atlanta and pursues non-capitalist ventures with human rights and environmental justice organizations and movements. She has studied classical Indian dance, in addition to engineering, and has an MFA from Bennington College. She has performed across the United States, and her poetry and nonfiction have appeared in many magazines and journals.

Muhammad Afzal Shahid is a poet and a scholar of classical Punjabi literature. He writes on contemporary themes in English, Urdu, and Punjabi and is the author of seven collections of Punjabi poetry. A physicist by training, he has worked at Carnegie Mellon University and at Bell Labs.

Amritjit Singh, Langston Hughes Professor of English at Ohio University, is a series editor for the MELA (Multi-Ethnic Literatures of the Americas) Series from Rutgers University Press. He has authored or co-edited over a dozen books, including *Postcolonial Theory and the United States* (2000), *The Collected Writings of Wallace Thurman* (2003), and *Interviews with Edward W. Said* (2004). His poems and translations from Punjabi poetry and fiction have appeared in the *Toronto Review*, *Nimrod*, the *Edinburgh Review*, *New Letters*, *Chelsea Magazine*, the *Salzburg Poetry Review*, and the *South Asian Review*.

Sher Zaman Taizi was born in Pabbi, in what was then the North-West Frontier Province of Pakistan. He has fifteen books in Pashto, including five novels, and twenty-four in English to his credit. He was awarded the Nobel Peace Prize Certificate in 1981 and the Tamgha-i-Imtiaz in Literature in 2009. He has done research and translation work in English relating to Afghan affairs.

Fakhar Zaman is the former Minister of Culture of Pakistan and former Chairman of the National Commission of History and Culture, the Academy of Letters, and the National Committee for the World Decade on Culture and Development. He is also the author of twenty-five books (novels, poetry, drama, and travelogues) written in Punjabi, Urdu, and English. Zaman has received several international awards and his books have been translated into various languages. He has also written many plays for TV and radio. Fakhar Zaman is presently chairman of the World Punjabi Congress as well as Secretary General of the International Congress of Writers, Artists and Intellectuals.

IFTIKHAR ARIF is an Urdu poet and scholar. He is currently the Chairman of Pakistan's National Language Authority and has received the Presidential Pride of Performance award. His poetry has been translated into several languages, including English in the collection *Written in a Season of Fear*.

WAQAS KHWAJA is a Professor of English at Agnes Scott College. He has published three collections of poetry and a travelogue, and has edited several anthologies of Pakistani literature.

PETROS ABATZOGLOU, *What Does Mrs. Freeman Want?*
MICHAL AJVAZ, *The Golden Age.*
The Other City.
PIERRE ALBERT-BIROT, *Grabinoulor.*
YUZ ALESHKOVSKY, *Kangaroo.*
FELIPE ALFAU, *Chromos.*
Locos.
IVAN ÂNGELO, *The Celebration.*
The Tower of Glass.
DAVID ANTIN, *Talking.*
ANTÓNIO LOBO ANTUNES, *Knowledge of Hell.*
ALAIN ARIAS-MISSON, *Theatre of Incest.*
IFTIKHAR ARIF AND WAQAS KHWAJA, EDS., *Modern Poetry of Pakistan.*
JOHN ASHBERY AND JAMES SCHUYLER, *A Nest of Ninnies.*
HEIMRAD BÄCKER, *transcript.*
DJUNA BARNES, *Ladies Almanack.*
Ryder.
JOHN BARTH, *LETTERS.*
Sabbatical.
DONALD BARTHELME, *The King.*
Paradise.
SVETISLAV BASARA, *Chinese Letter.*
RENÉ BELLETTO, *Dying.*
MARK BINELLI, *Sacco and Vanzetti Must Die!*
ANDREI BITOV, *Pushkin House.*
ANDREJ BLATNIK, *You Do Understand.*
LOUIS PAUL BOON, *Chapel Road.*
My Little War.
Summer in Termuren.
ROGER BOYLAN, *Killoyle.*
IGNÁCIO DE LOYOLA BRANDÃO, *Anonymous Celebrity.*
The Good-Bye Angel.
Teeth under the Sun.
Zero.
BONNIE BREMSER, *Troia: Mexican Memoirs.*
CHRISTINE BROOKE-ROSE, *Amalgamemnon.*
BRIGID BROPHY, *In Transit.*
MEREDITH BROSNAN, *Mr. Dynamite.*
GERALD L. BRUNS, *Modern Poetry and the Idea of Language.*
EVGENY BUNIMOVICH AND J. KATES, EDS., *Contemporary Russian Poetry: An Anthology.*
GABRIELLE BURTON, *Heartbreak Hotel.*
MICHEL BUTOR, *Degrees.*
Mobile.
Portrait of the Artist as a Young Ape.
G. CABRERA INFANTE, *Infante's Inferno.*
Three Trapped Tigers.
JULIETA CAMPOS, *The Fear of Losing Eurydice.*
ANNE CARSON, *Eros the Bittersweet.*
ORLY CASTEL-BLOOM, *Dolly City.*
CAMILO JOSÉ CELA, *Christ versus Arizona.*
The Family of Pascual Duarte.
The Hive.
LOUIS-FERDINAND CÉLINE, *Castle to Castle.*
Conversations with Professor Y.
London Bridge.
Normance.
North.
Rigadoon.
HUGO CHARTERIS, *The Tide Is Right.*
JEROME CHARYN, *The Tar Baby.*
MARC CHOLODENKO, *Mordechai Schamz.*
JOSHUA COHEN, *Witz.*
EMILY HOLMES COLEMAN, *The Shutter of Snow.*
ROBERT COOVER, *A Night at the Movies.*
STANLEY CRAWFORD, *Log of the S.S. The Mrs Unguentine.*
Some Instructions to My Wife.
ROBERT CREELEY, *Collected Prose.*
RENÉ CREVEL, *Putting My Foot in It.*
RALPH CUSACK, *Cadenza.*
SUSAN DAITCH, *L.C.*
Storytown.
NICHOLAS DELBANCO, *The Count of Concord.*
NIGEL DENNIS, *Cards of Identity.*
PETER DIMOCK, *A Short Rhetoric for Leaving the Family.*
ARIEL DORFMAN, *Konfidenz.*
COLEMAN DOWELL, *The Houses of Children.*
Island People.
Too Much Flesh and Jabez.
ARKADII DRAGOMOSHCHENKO, *Dust.*
RIKKI DUCORNET, *The Complete Butcher's Tales.*
The Fountains of Neptune.
The Jade Cabinet.
The One Marvelous Thing.
Phosphor in Dreamland.
The Stain.
The Word "Desire."
WILLIAM EASTLAKE, *The Bamboo Bed.*
Castle Keep.
Lyric of the Circle Heart.
JEAN ECHENOZ, *Chopin's Move.*
STANLEY ELKIN, *A Bad Man.*
Boswell: A Modern Comedy.
Criers and Kibitzers, Kibitzers and Criers.
The Dick Gibson Show.
The Franchiser.
George Mills.
The Living End.
The MacGuffin.
The Magic Kingdom.
Mrs. Ted Bliss.
The Rabbi of Lud.
Van Gogh's Room at Arles.
ANNIE ERNAUX, *Cleaned Out.*
LAUREN FAIRBANKS, *Muzzle Thyself.*
Sister Carrie.
LESLIE A. FIEDLER, *Love and Death in the American Novel.*
JUAN FILLOY, *Op Oloop.*
GUSTAVE FLAUBERT, *Bouvard and Pécuchet.*
KASS FLEISHER, *Talking out of School.*
FORD MADOX FORD, *The March of Literature.*
JON FOSSE, *Aliss at the Fire.*
Melancholy.

My Life in CIA.
Singular Pleasures.
The Sinking of the Odradek
Stadium.
Tlooth.
20 Lines a Day.
JOSEPH MCELROY,
Night Soul and Other Stories.
ROBERT L. MCLAUGHLIN, ED.,
Innovations: An Anthology of
Modern & Contemporary Fiction.
HERMAN MELVILLE, *The Confidence-Man.*
AMANDA MICHALOPOULOU, *I'd Like.*
STEVEN MILLHAUSER,
The Barnum Museum.
In the Penny Arcade.
RALPH J. MILLS, JR.,
Essays on Poetry.
MOMUS, *The Book of Jokes.*
CHRISTINE MONTALBETTI, *Western.*
OLIVE MOORE, *Spleen.*
NICHOLAS MOSLEY, *Accident.*
Assassins.
Catastrophe Practice.
Children of Darkness and Light.
Experience and Religion.
God's Hazard.
The Hesperides Tree.
Hopeful Monsters.
Imago Bird.
Impossible Object.
Inventing God.
Judith.
Look at the Dark.
Natalie Natalia.
Paradoxes of Peace.
Serpent.
Time at War.
The Uses of Slime Mould:
Essays of Four Decades.
WARREN MOTTE,
Fables of the Novel: French Fiction
since 1990.
Fiction Now: The French Novel in
the 21st Century.
Oulipo: A Primer of Potential
Literature.
YVES NAVARRE, *Our Share of Time.*
Sweet Tooth.
DOROTHY NELSON, *In Night's City.*
Tar and Feathers.
ESHKOL NEVO, *Homesick.*
WILFRIDO D. NOLLEDO,
But for the Lovers.
FLANN O'BRIEN,
At Swim-Two-Birds.
At War.
The Best of Myles.
The Dalkey Archive.
Further Cuttings.
The Hard Life.
The Poor Mouth.
The Third Policeman.
CLAUDE OLLIER, *The Mise-en-Scène.*
PATRIK OUŘEDNÍK, *Europeana.*
BORIS PAHOR, *Necropolis.*

FERNANDO DEL PASO,
News from the Empire.
Palinuro of Mexico.
ROBERT PINGET, *The Inquisitory.*
Mahu or The Material.
Trio.
MANUEL PUIG,
Betrayed by Rita Hayworth.
The Buenos Aires Affair.
Heartbreak Tango.
RAYMOND QUENEAU, *The Last Days.*
Odile.
Pierrot Mon Ami.
Saint Glinglin.
ANN QUIN, *Berg.*
Passages.
Three.
Tripticks.
ISHMAEL REED,
The Free-Lance Pallbearers.
The Last Days of Louisiana Red.
Ishmael Reed: The Plays.
Reckless Eyeballing.
The Terrible Threes.
The Terrible Twos.
Yellow Back Radio Broke-Down.
JEAN RICARDOU, *Place Names.*
RAINER MARIA RILKE, *The Notebooks of*
Malte Laurids Brigge.
JULIÁN RÍOS, *The House of Ulysses.*
Larva: A Midsummer Night's Babel.
Poundemonium.
AUGUSTO ROA BASTOS, *I the Supreme.*
DANIËL ROBBERECHTS,
Arriving in Avignon.
OLIVIER ROLIN, *Hotel Crystal.*
ALIX CLEO ROUBAUD, *Alix's Journal.*
JACQUES ROUBAUD, *The Form of a*
City Changes Faster, Alas, Than
the Human Heart.
The Great Fire of London.
Hortense in Exile.
Hortense Is Abducted.
The Loop.
The Plurality of Worlds of Lewis.
The Princess Hoppy.
Some Thing Black.
LEON S. ROUDIEZ,
French Fiction Revisited.
VEDRANA RUDAN, *Night.*
STIG SÆTERBAKKEN, *Siamese.*
LYDIE SALVAYRE, *The Company of Ghosts.*
Everyday Life.
The Lecture.
Portrait of the Writer as a
Domesticated Animal.
The Power of Flies.
LUIS RAFAEL SÁNCHEZ,
Macho Camacho's Beat.
SEVERO SARDUY, *Cobra & Maitreya.*
NATHALIE SARRAUTE,
Do You Hear Them?
Martereau.
The Planetarium.
ARNO SCHMIDT, *Collected Stories.*
Nobodaddy's Children.

CHRISTINE SCHUTT, *Nightwork.*
GAIL SCOTT, *My Paris.*
DAMION SEARLS, *What We Were Doing and Where We Were Going.*
JUNE AKERS SEESE,
Is This What Other Women Feel Too?
What Waiting Really Means.
BERNARD SHARE, *Inish.*
Transit.
AURELIE SHEEHAN,
Jack Kerouac Is Pregnant.
VIKTOR SHKLOVSKY, *Knight's Move.*
A Sentimental Journey: Memoirs 1917–1922.
Energy of Delusion: A Book on Plot.
Literature and Cinematography.
Theory of Prose.
Third Factory.
Zoo, or Letters Not about Love.
CLAUDE SIMON, *The Invitation.*
PIERRE SINIAC, *The Collaborators.*
JOSEF ŠKVORECKÝ, *The Engineer of Human Souls.*
GILBERT SORRENTINO,
Aberration of Starlight.
Blue Pastoral.
Crystal Vision.
Imaginative Qualities of Actual Things.
Mulligan Stew.
Pack of Lies.
Red the Fiend.
The Sky Changes.
Something Said.
Splendide-Hôtel.
Steelwork.
Under the Shadow.
W. M. SPACKMAN,
The Complete Fiction.
ANDRZEJ STASIUK, *Fado.*
GERTRUDE STEIN,
Lucy Church Amiably.
The Making of Americans.
A Novel of Thank You.
LARS SVENDSEN, *A Philosophy of Evil.*
PIOTR SZEWC, *Annihilation.*
GONÇALO M. TAVARES, *Jerusalem.*
LUCIAN DAN TEODOROVICI,
Our Circus Presents . . .
STEFAN THEMERSON, *Hobson's Island.*
The Mystery of the Sardine.
Tom Harris.
JOHN TOOMEY, *Sleepwalker.*
JEAN-PHILIPPE TOUSSAINT,
The Bathroom.
Camera.
Monsieur.
Running Away.
Self-Portrait Abroad.
Television.
DUMITRU TSEPENEAG,
Hotel Europa.
The Necessary Marriage.
Pigeon Post.
Vain Art of the Fugue.
ESTHER TUSQUETS, *Stranded.*

DUBRAVKA UGRESIC,
Lend Me Your Character.
Thank You for Not Reading.
MATI UNT, *Brecht at Night.*
Diary of a Blood Donor.
Things in the Night.
ÁLVARO URIBE AND OLIVIA SEARS, EDS.,
Best of Contemporary Mexican Fiction.
ELOY URROZ, *Friction.*
The Obstacles.
LUISA VALENZUELA, *He Who Searches.*
MARJA-LIISA VARTIO,
The Parson's Widow.
PAUL VERHAEGHEN, *Omega Minor.*
BORIS VIAN, *Heartsnatcher.*
LLORENÇ VILLALONGA, *The Dolls' Room.*
ORNELA VORPSI, *The Country Where No One Ever Dies.*
AUSTRYN WAINHOUSE, *Hedyphagetica.*
PAUL WEST,
Words for a Deaf Daughter & Gala.
CURTIS WHITE,
America's Magic Mountain.
The Idea of Home.
Memories of My Father Watching TV.
Monstrous Possibility: An Invitation to Literary Politics.
Requiem.
DIANE WILLIAMS, *Excitability: Selected Stories.*
Romancer Erector.
DOUGLAS WOOLF, *Wall to Wall.*
Ya! & John-Juan.
JAY WRIGHT, *Polynomials and Pollen.*
The Presentable Art of Reading Absence.
PHILIP WYLIE, *Generation of Vipers.*
MARGUERITE YOUNG,
Angel in the Forest.
Miss MacIntosh, My Darling.
REYOUNG, *Unbabbling.*
VLADO ŽABOT, *The Succubus.*
ZORAN ŽIVKOVIĆ, *Hidden Camera.*
LOUIS ZUKOFSKY, *Collected Fiction.*
SCOTT ZWIREN, *God Head.*